To Thessalonians with Love

TO THESSALONIANS WITH LOVE

John D. Hendrix

BROADMAN PRESS
Nashville, Tennessee

Unless otherwise noted, Scripture quotations are from the Revised Standard Version of the Bible, copyrighted 1946, 1952, © 1971, 1973.

Scripture quotations marked (KJV) are from the King James Version of the Bible.

Scripture quotations marked (Moffatt) are from *The Bible: a New Translation* by James A. R. Moffatt. Copyright © 1935 by Harper and Row, Publishers, Inc. Used by permission.

Scripture quotations marked (NEB) are from *The New English Bible*. Copyright © The Delegates of the Oxford University Press and the Syndics of the Cambridge University Press, 1961, 1970. Reprinted by permission.

Scripture quotations marked (Phillips) are reprinted with permission of the Macmillan Publishing Co., Inc. from J. B. Phillips: *The New Testament in Modern English*, Revised Edition. © J. B. Phillips 1958, 1960, 1972.

Scripture quotations marked (TLB) are taken from *The Living Bible*. Copyright © Tyndale House Publishers, Wheaton, Illinois, 1971. Used by permission.

© Copyright 1982 • Broadman Press
All rights reserved.
4213-12
ISBN: 0-8054-1312-X
Dewey Decimal Classification: 227.81
Subject Heading: BIBLE. N.T. 1 THESSALONIANS
Library of Congress Catalog Card Number: 81-70974
Printed in the United States of America

To Lela
"You are the one."
1 Thessalonians 2:20

Preface

This book has been a long time coming. The experiences in my life that revolved around 1 Thessalonians 2:7-8 happened in 1965-1966. In some way I have been writing this book ever since those events. So, I have been a Jacob, struggling with something from heaven that would not let me go. The learning model is the best way I have found to make sense of the struggle.

I am not a Bible scholar. But I would like to be an interpreter of the Bible and the human condition. The fact is, 1 Thessalonians is the only book of the Bible that I know in the way I define "knowing." This book knew me before I knew myself, and I have never grown tired of it. Before I became an interpreter, 1 Thessalonians interpreted me. It continues to be the primary resource in shaping much of my thinking and reflecting. I hope that those who know me best will say, "Yep, that's him all right!"

There is always the temptation to write to peers and colleagues. I have tried to avoid that and write directly to the people. They have kept me working at clarifying the message. From their responses I know that I have touched a nerve.

First Thessalonians talks about a work to do and a people to love. Happily, I have found that good mix in the Church Training Department of the Baptist Sunday School Board. I express appreciation to them and to Broadman for stirring up the fires.

Contents

Introduction

In 1970 James Smart wrote *The Strange Silence of the Bible in the Churches*. The dilemma that he saw the churches facing with the Bible still has a prophetic ring of truth.

> Any open attack upon the Bible as a whole, or even upon the Old Testament portion of it, or any attempt to reduce it to a subordinate status in the church, would undoubtedly meet with almost universal resistance. But let the deed be done unobtrusively, not by any concerted plan of any faction but as the result of factors that are at work unconsciously in all of us, and let the surface appearance be maintained so that what has been happening below the surface escapes the notice of most people, and we could awaken one day to find ourselves a church almost totally alienated from the Scriptures.[1]

The two key words here are *unconscious* and *alienation*. In simpler terms they mean emotional distance. The Christian's relationship to the Bible is in trouble. There is attachment without closeness, commitment without warmth, intellectual involvement without intimacy, togetherness without fun. It is a marriage all right, but a bad one.

Many Christians are attached to the Bible by an invisible ten-foot pole which joins them and keeps them apart. The pole has been constructed through years of the dry, lifeless recounting of biblical material unrelated and irrelevant to the deep needs of the heart. In this strange and bizarre position, the Christian maneuvers—swinging, punching, jabbing—keeping others away but unable to bring the living Word any closer.

Three experiences have led me to these conclusions. The first was the personal encounter with 1 Thessalonians 2:7-8 at a time when I desperately needed some way of interpreting my experiences. My romance with that letter has never ended. I will attempt to clarify that experience in the commentary.

The second has been the struggle of designing learning experiences for adults and youth in Christian education. I have been through it all—developmental needs, learning readinesses, behavioral outcomes, contemporary issues—you name it. But something was lacking. I simply did not know enough about the radical nature of the human condition. There was always the feeling that the center of the design was inadequate, no matter how much I surrounded and buttressed it with the biblical material.

Finally, I have listened to the message of the churches. How does the Word of God do its "work" in personal and corporate church life? I have listened for that through countless sermons, Bible studies, small-group discussions, and personal conversations. And there is the strange silence.

There are moments of reflection which are vaguely connected with a biblical phrase, sentence, verse, or book. Many discourses have the appearance of drawing from the biblical text. But, in reality, they are topical exercises, a cafeteria of "junk foods," full of artificial preservatives and additives, providing no nutritional value and an abundance of hyperactivity. I have been listening for that transforming moment when a body of Scripture (a unit, paragraph, or text) actually touches the inner depths of a personal struggle.

It is simply not there. Or it is such a private experience that it cannot be expressed in a way that is helpful to others. The Bible is primarily a public book to be read, proclaimed, and interpreted in the presence of others. Like most of Paul's letters, 1 Thessalonians is directed to a church. Bible study loses much of its force unless it is spoken and heard in the company of God's people.

I am not addressing the issues of inspiration, interpretation, and inerrancy. I am addressing the issue of intimacy—personal and interpersonal closeness to the biblical text in daily life. Unconscious alienation from the Bible is present in churches of all theological persuasions.

Intimacy with Scripture

My experience says that most of us have great uncertainty in working with Scripture at an intimate level. This is not a matter of humanistic rejection of the authority and power of Scripture. It is not a matter of liberal or conservative perspective, for the same thing is true along all lines of the theological continuum. It is rather an emotional strangeness, a sense of distance that does not make it available to daily experience. The Scripture is solid, not fluid. We see it, look at it, but cannot get into it. Our view of Scripture is like standing on the shore looking at a body of water. We soon grow weary of it without ever experiencing the marvelous life that lies beneath the surface.

The crucial question remains in how intimately we deal with the text. No matter how much lip service and respect is given to the biblical text, it still remains distant from the lives of many people. In our most crucial specific life situations, we find Scripture irrelevant, unhelpful, or unapproachable. We have neither the tools nor the time to learn it. Our training has given us an appreciation for Scripture without the skills of access to it. I am looking for a warm friendliness with Scripture, an increase in intimacy and closeness, a lively presence of Scripture in the midst of our life together.

For many of us the Christian language is no longer revelatory. Since this has happened, we are faced with the enormous task of giving new body to it. This does not happen through merely intellectual and rational reordering and rearranging. Rather, it happens through the "mix" of experience with Scripture which "images" the life and blood of truth—the whole person encountering the Word of God.

There is the old story of someone born blind having to have explained to him what the color scarlet is by his being told that it is like the sound of a trumpet. Whether that is a happy analogy or not, it is plain that the only possible way in which a person born blind can be given any information regarding color is by the use of some things within his own experience.

The letters of Paul speak to our experience. Paul does not teach us a lesson. Rather, we are invited into his life. This personal encounter is the power of Scripture for my life now. It is not once upon a time; it is every time a person gets caught up in it and by it.

We become participants not because we want to necessarily or because we have "gotten the point." For a moment we have lost control. We have been interpreted. The secure, familiar everydayness of our lives has been opened up and seen in another way. Our response is more like an infusion of new blood than it is like a piece of information to be stored in the head.

Why are autobiographies and personal documents so interesting to read? The reason is that we reflect on our lives as we read about another's life. Our interest in the life stories of others stems from fascination with our own stories. We read autobiographies in order to find out about ourselves. In other words, in the midst of whatever other questions are raised, one first and foremost raises the question of oneself.

Paul's letters challenge us much like an autobiography. A letter is a form between the parable and the confession. It keeps the writer and the world in solution because it is written out of the writer's experience and utilizes that experience in a personal way. Paul not only used himself but also thought in and through himself. He took himself as a human metaphor. He thought with his blood. He was in the midst of his own struggle (1 Thess. 2:8). He lived that which he attempted to convey. His words were "inspired," breathed into by God and hammered out through the agony and passion of his own life.

A Learning Model

In Bible study we need both a unifying model and a practical way of using it. Intimacy with Scripture occurs when we are grabbed by something in our experience as it relates to a biblical text, look back at that experience in a reflective manner, draw some personal insights, and risk these insights in a practical way. This process is often experienced in everyone's ordinary living and learning. Learning can be defined as a relatively stable but permanent change (transformation) that results from experience, biblical exegesis, reflection, and application.

This book uses a model of learning applied to Bible study. The model is not always evident, but it is always there as a design for involving persons in the biblical text. I hope you will not notice the passage from one part of the process to another. However, each part of the process has its own essential roles and development.

Experience

In the beginning is the explosive, powerful, transforming experience that comes with a confrontation with divine truth. Faith comes before understanding. We proclaim an experiential faith. "That . . . which we have heard, which we have seen with our eyes, which we have looked upon and touched with our hands, concerning the word of life—the life was made manifest, and we saw it, and testify to it, and proclaim to you" (1 John 1:1-2).

Paul's faith was an experiential faith. When we stand on the primacy of our faith experience, we stand with Paul.

> Paul never ceased to believe that he was loyal to the traditions of his fathers, but he insisted on interpreting those traditions in the light of his overpowering experience of the Risen Christ at Damascus. Paul resolved the conflict between experience and tradition in favor of the authority of his own experience.[2]

The authority of experience comes in what we make of our own private and personal pasts rather than what comes from our public pasts. It is what we have always loved, what we have always hated, what is still eating on us one way or another after many years, that carries impact. In these experiences we really know with the heart rather than with the head. What I know does not necessarily spring out of the facts of my life, that can be written on a resumé, but those things that are intimately wedded to me—my concerns, turbulences, loves, hopes, and sorrows.

We need not be frightened by our experiences. Our fears come from the feeling that *this has happened to me only, and no one will understand.* The opposite is true. I first encountered this in a maxim by Carl Rogers: "What is most personal is most general." What a surprise! I have found that those feelings that seem to be most private and personal are those which are most common. When clearly expressed, they resonate deeply and consistently with the experiences of others. What I experience in a unique and personal way is somehow mirrored in the experiences of others. The response is, "I know something about that. I've just never heard anyone talk about it before."

This is the reality that underlies biblical truth. Behind the truth is an experience. Martin Luther's words "I did not find my theology all at once, but I had to search for it where my temptations took me" are rediscovered in every person's experience. There is always a need for encountering the depth of the Scripture in the reality of life.

When we speak from experience, we speak from the center of Baptist thought. An experiential faith sets a personal encounter boldly to the front. Churches are composed on the basis of the Christian experience of their members. Believers' baptism is practiced because it has an experience to back it up. A prerequisite to ministry is the Christian experience of conversion. We want to know about conversions, about calls. These are examples of Baptist insistence that a personal experience with God is a necessary qualification for Christian service.

Exegesis

Experience looks to Scripture for interpretation. *How do I make sense out of what has happened to me?* The Christian faith says, "Look at God's Word." This is not a subjective look but a specific, accurate, precise interpretation of a biblical truth. The meaning of Scripture is rooted out and stated in an orderly fashion. We wrestle with the meaning of the biblical text, fixing it in our minds in such a way as to leave an indelible imprint. Reading or referring to Scripture does not have the same effect. It lacks that inward digesting that makes it part of us. Nothing can take the place of doing our homework on the biblical text.

Exegesis is working with the sequence of the text. The Bible is not a loose-jointed fitting together of random individual texts. Rather, Scripture is a close-knit unit, with definite growth and development of ideas within a passage and from one passage to the next. Scripture is a growing tree with all parts developmentally related rather than a mosaic of random, unconnected elements. Words and phrases are known by the company they keep. In many cases, a development of sequence can come directly from the biblical text. In other words, the best study of Scripture is often verse by verse.

The learning process is an extremely inaccurate hit-and-miss operation. So we let Scripture shape its own message. The development of the text in orderly form gives shape to an otherwise chaotic learning process. The best route to follow is usually the one that parallels the text.

Exegesis is working with images and word pictures. Images are often used in Scripture to convey profound spiritual truths. Images will tell us what a truth is like in language that we can understand. Biblical language is graphic, pictorial, and unusual language. Biblical language is meant to touch us deeply, uniting the concrete and the abstract, the emotional and the mental, the subjective and the objective. The Bible is full of metaphors and similes that can provide our teaching with emotional qualities.

Exegesis is working with words. Through the words in the Bible, God reveals himself. We learn from God by studying the *words* of the Bible. The separate study of individual words opens up a gold mine of material. The ultimate purpose is not to study linguistics but to study revelation, not to learn Hebrew or Greek but to learn the mind of God and respond to his Word. In word study, we can search out the depth which one passage of Scripture owes to another one.

This careful and precise documentation of biblical material is essential to the learning process. An exegesis of Scripture, done accurately and in-depth, prevents our reading into the text what we want it to say. A lesson can be learned from the German theologian, Karl Barth. When the Nazis no longer permitted him to lecture at the University of Bonn, he left the lecture room by shouting, "Exegesis, exegesis, exegesis!" What he meant was that the German nation was being bewitched by a special brew of Nazi ideology and Christian theology. Many times in his earlier years, Hitler would stand before an audience with a Bible open in his hands, claiming that he was saying nothing more than what was in the Bible, which the audience had learned at their mothers' knees. If the German Christians were to unmask the bewitching Nazi religion, it could only be done by a continuing accurate study of Scripture. This was the meaning of Barth's crying, "Exegesis, exegesis, exegesis!"

And so it is. If we are to remain true to biblical truth, we cannot be seed pickers in the theological market or easy victims of theological spellbinders. Only as we are deeply steeped in Scripture can we prevent ourselves from being victims of every current fad and novelty.

Reflection

Reflection holds personal experience and biblical truth "in solution." We begin to mix the biblical text with our life situations. Through reflection we begin to hear the Word that is somehow hidden in the words.

Reflection begins the talking process. We hear ourselves say things we have never said before. We publish (make publicly known) those things that are ruminating in our minds and hearts. We "chew the cud"—recalling, remembering, pondering, refusing to let it go. Reflection requires a deliberate and disciplined effort to stop the action long enough to ask, What is going on? What am I beginning to learn? What is different about me?

The reflective process demands a mental shift from verbal, logical thinking to a more feeling, intuitive mode of thinking. Learning how to see means a good deal more than merely looking with the eyes. The Bible is the means through which all of life can be seen. No experience is seen in a vacuum apart from Scripture. It is a peculiar lens radically different from other perspectives. It calls into question every other way of viewing life.

Reflection invites us to a different way of knowing, understanding, and deciding. We become more inventive, searching, daring, and self-expressive. We become more interested in other people. When others try to close the book on truth, we continue to open it. There are still more pages to be written.

When we hold the Bible and our lives in solution, we discover that they are one and the same world. The Bible becomes a mirror through which we see ourselves and others. Only in reflection does the Bible become transparent. Far too often we look into the Bible and see only what is in the Bible. This is another way of saying that we have not seen past the words to the Word of God. The Bible has the power to transform only as we see past the words to the living Word.

The Word upsets the old logic of everydayness. The new logic of grace begins to move in. It is not a matter of making the text relevant. The text is relevant—it calls for response. What is happening to you? What do you say? What will you do?

There is a new way of believing and living that initially seems ordinary. But, as the Scripture works in us, we find ourselves moved from our usual contexts of living to a different way of living. It is not that we have learned our lesson. The everydayness of our lives has been torn apart. We see another story. The habitual rhythms of our lives move to a different beat, and we begin to understand with our hearts' blood rather than with just our heads. We are shocked by revelation. Like the parables of Jesus, extraordinary things happen to ordinary lives.

Transformation is a shift, a break with continuity, the introduction of something new. The grace of God breaks in and is not something familiar or understandable in terms of our previous experiences. God's grace—we cannot see it or touch it. We have no way of measuring it. Yet, this grace continues to operate as the most powerful force in human life. Hence, the need for reflection. What's going on here, anyway?

Application

Our encounter with Scripture is like a punch to the midsection. For a moment, it takes our breath away. One thing is certain. It will get us moving. Application is both opportunity and motivation to test our learning in specific daily situations. Since the old logic of living is no longer operative, application usually involves risk. That makes application both frightening and exciting. Applying the Scripture calls for a response that is both personal and unique. None of us can dare decide what responses others will make. There is no way of knowing what transforming experiences will lead people to do. Be ready for surprise!

The black congregations of central Missouri have a way of reminding their preachers about applying the text. You can feel it coming. Finally, they can contain the need no longer. "Bring it home, Pastor!" they shout. The application of Scripture is putting it to the test—bringing it home.

Our attraction to Scripture implies application. Our desire to apply leads us to the pages of the Bible. The application of the text is not step 4 in the learning process. Understanding the text is already applying it. Understanding only comes in the ability to practice (as in mathematics). True knowledge lies in our ability to use it. If that is true of mathematics, how much more should it be true of biblical faith, which is always challenging us to convert learning into living.

Processing the Learning Model

The learning model can be described with a simple diagram.

Each line represents a way of knowing. The horizontal arrows (exegesis—application) analyze, abstract, direct, think, plan, verbalize, reason, sequence, and figure it out. The vertical arrows (experience—

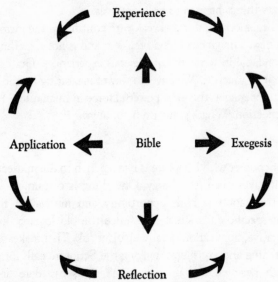

reflection) imagine, vision, dream, feel, relate, gesture, sense, and get the picture. (For a more complete analysis of the learning model see the Appendix.)

This is not a step-by-step learning process. Learning may start anywhere and go in any direction. That is the dynamic that makes the learning process imprecise and chaotic. But the model does provide boundaries, and learning breaks down if all four areas are not entered at some time.

The Bible lives at the center of the process. The "ways of knowing" move around and through the center. The biblical core informs and transforms all the ways of knowing. The living Word operates within the process and outside the process, working within and breaking in, making all things new.

All models are inadequate, but they do provide a framework for learning. Since transforming kinds of learning are unpredictable and capricious, a model provides some structure. The model cannot explain transformation, but it does provide some handles for processing it. By placing learning in some kind of framework, we are freed for an intensity of involvement.

Once or twice a week I participate in an activity that appears to be very restricting. The room is totally enclosed with four walls and a high ceiling. There are no windows and the only door fades into the back wall. There is nothing in the room. Only some painted lines break the monotony of walls, floor, and ceiling. Do you feel the restrictions? If it is a prison, the answer is yes. But what if the room is a racquetball court? Now the limitations are exciting, intense, and exhilarating. The confining walls make the movement of the ball enormously challenging. So it is with unpredictable learning that is provided a framework.

Yet there is more. The model provides a structure for the Holy Spirit to embody. We do not control the Holy Spirit with a framework. Rather, we provide God's Spirit with an arena to "fill up" with grace. By building a frame, we offer him something to work with, knowing all the time that the wind of God's Spirit "blows where it will."

Let's look at the model in a different way. Take an eight-to-ten–inch slip of paper one-inch wide and draw a line along one side. Call that line "thinking and doing." In our model that is the horizontal line of exegesis and application. Turn the sheet over and draw another line. Call that line "sensing and feeling." In our model that is the vertical line of experience and reflection. The two sides represent two separate and distinct ways of knowing and understanding Scripture. Now twist the paper and join the ends. You now have one unending line, joined and blended together in unity. The cognitive (thinking) and the affective (feeling) are confluent (flowing together). That is another way of picturing a process that the Holy Spirit can use in bringing us to an intimate relationship with Holy Scripture.

To Thessalonians with Love

We know the difference between a business letter (no matter how fancy it is) and a genuine personal communication. The contrast is evident in an intimate love letter and correspondence addressed "To whom it may concern." The intimate letter is full of personal references. To reach the heart of the people addressed, communication must be true "co-respondence." That is, the communication calls for a genuine response from the others in the communication. But even personal references in second- and third-class mail often lack meaning. We all know that from Christmas letters! The secret to Paul's letters is that they come to each of us first class, as if they were sent to us and us alone, true heart-to-heart communication. "To Thessalonians with love" is somehow Paul's love letter to each one of us.

In this book, I attempt to describe my relationship to Paul through one of his letters. My experience is a primal witness and perhaps has greater value for me than any interpretations others wish to put on it. But my own experience is the only form which can be real or valid for me. It is the way I see things and the observations I make about these perceptions at this particular time in my life. As someone has said, "You can see a whole lot just by looking." This is the way I have looked at 1 Thessalonians.

In Paul's letter to the Thessalonians, those in the relationship know the real meaning behind the words. There is a power and significance in the words and beyond the words that only those in the relationship can see. In the words and between the words of this letter, I was able to make sense of some of my own critical life situations.

An Interpersonal Commentary

First Thessalonians is probably the first piece of Christian literature to come down to us. It is "pure Paul," written before his writing style reached those later lofty heights. His words provide much emotional content, carrying hints of the intimate nature of his relationship with these people. The style is simple and unhurried, providing simple instructions and exhortations about interpersonal living.

Paul combined humility and confidence, strong fortitude and enthusiasm, and an unfailing perseverance. Although he hit the lows, the highs were not far in coming. Emotionally, he bounced. We find him on a roller coaster of rapidly changing feelings.

First Thessalonians provides us a good model of interpersonal Bible study because of two themes that keep recurring in the letter. One is the "grace-full" message which is to be communicated. The other is Paul's transparent sharing of his own life with these people.

First Thessalonians found me at a time of intense interpersonal need. The more I live with it, the more its central meaning becomes clear. First

Thessalonians proclaims the principles of Christian interpersonal life, and it is expressed in the words and between the words of an extremely personal letter. Although there are other letters that offer some revealing insights about Paul's emotional and interpersonal life, none shows the depth of 1 Thessalonians. I am ready to take a stand on that. And I am ready to address that specific theme.

Paul opened his heart to this young church. He assured them that he loved them dearly and longed to see them again. He beseeched and exhorted, warned and rebuked. He comforted, assured, and encouraged. He "really lived" only if they stood fast. Most of all, he expressed joy and thanksgiving for what they meant to his life.

First Thessalonians 2:19-20 provides us with the central truth. Paul said, in verse 19, "Is it not you?" Who could it be if it is "not you?" Paul gave them a special place in his life. In verse 20, the emphasis is on both *you* and *are*. The Thessalonians (and *no other*) were (and not *would be*) his pride and joy.

The letter was written out of Paul's own need to the significant people in his life. He shared the intimate things of his heart for all the world to see. That is also my purpose in writing.

1
How Relationships Begin
1:1-10

Saying Hello (1:1)

Greetings are usually short but significant. Some have said that the first four minutes in a relationship will tell the story. That is not always true, but it points to the importance of starting a relationship well. For those people we know well, a short greeting is all that is necessary. We can pick up where we left off. There is no need for formal titles, flowery introductions, and proper niceties.

The greeting in 1 Thessalonians is the shortest of all Paul's writings, but it contains all that is essential and implies an intimate relationship. It is not much more than a "Hi!" It carries a note of affection rather than authority. Paul, Silvanus, and Timothy were all on friendly terms with the church. All three were personally known and loved.

This letter, like 2 Thessalonians, is addressed to "the church of Thessalonians," a form of address not used elsewhere. Why should this one church be addressed differently from all of the others? There is no article *the* before "Thessalonians" in the Greek. The letter was not addressed to all of the Thessalonians, only to those Thessalonians who made up the church. This gives us the first hint that the letter is personal and intimate. Paul's emphasis was on the people in the church rather than on those in the city or the country. The church was small. He probably knew each member by name. His relationship with them was special.

Grace to You (1:1)

"Grace to you" is the first step in interpersonal communication. Yet these words often pass glibly by the lips of those reading Scripture. Paul began many of his letters with some form of this greeting. For us these words have become like fragile, antique vases, prized for their beauty more

27

than for their use. They have become empty of significance or meaning. But for Paul, the greeting was much more than a formality. Behind it was a rich background of Old Testament images and actions. Because it became the dominant greeting in Paul's writings, it deserves a more thorough examination.

A Simple Greeting. In 1 Thessalonians 1:1-2, we have this greeting in its earliest and simplest form. Here it was combined with the Jewish greeting "peace." The simplicity of the greeting which Paul extended to the Thessalonian church provides a clue to their relationship. A brief word would do because it carried the memories of past events. Although there are many other salutations in the Scriptures, this one is of Paul's own coinage—a special form in which he fused the very essence of his thought and conviction—grace to you.

"Grace to you" means that God is constantly giving us unearned favors. Because of grace, the Beatitudes of Jesus take on added significance. The poor, the mourning, the meek, and the persecuted can be called blessed because of grace. We are lost until grace finds us, undone until grace binds us up, burdened until grace enlightens us. We are weak until grace strengthens us, hungry until grace fills us, despairing until grace comforts us.

"Grace to you" is the response of God's people to the world's people. Grace to the stranger, the alien, the enemy. Grace to the guilty criminal. Grace to the morally bankrupt. Grace to the slave without money to buy freedom. Grace to the orphan. Grace to the distressed and disturbed. Grace finds us poor and makes us rich. Grace and grace alone is sufficient.

Setting the Heart Free. "Grace to you" began my journey toward interpersonal openness. Before "grace to you," there was bondage, seeking approval, avoiding the deeper meanings of my life, out of the fear that people would no longer like me.

That was especially true in my relationship with Lela. I will never forget that first attempt at sharing the secrets of my inner life. I kept thinking, *If she ever discovers who I really am she will not love me.* The words hung there in the darkness. How strange they sounded! I was hearing myself verbalize thoughts and feelings I had only spoken to myself for years. But when I finally got started, I couldn't stop. The feelings tumbled out for over an hour. Then I waited in the silent darkness to see how she would respond.

I never understood the meaning of grace until that night. I had heard sermons on grace and preached sermons on grace. I had outlined grace and exegeted grace. I had written about grace and sung about grace. But the next morning I knew that grace had been spoken to me, communicated in a touch, and affirmed through words. The spoken word of grace actually brought the grace of God. The next morning I was somehow different, clothed in the love of God and in my right mind. I really could be me, express my thoughts and feelings with confidence, without fearing that love would be taken away.

All my desperate but logical attempts to change up to that time had not worked. Grace came as transforming event—unpredictable, unplanned, abrupt, and illogical. Grace came breaking in from the outside and was not something familiar or understandable in terms of my previous experience.

Helen Keller's experience of learning is portrayed in a dramatic way for all of us. She could spell the word *water* through the fingertips of her teacher. She also knew the taste and touch of water and its life-renewing powers. But she had never connected the two until that day when the water poured over her hands in the midst of her anger and frustration. Suddenly, dramatically, and spontaneously it all came together. The word W-A-T-E-R described that cold, wet stuff that brought vigor and pleasure to her life. Perhaps in a less dramatic, but no less significant way, that was my experience in understanding grace.

A *Blessing*. What was behind Paul's greeting of grace and peace? Perhaps Paul was reminded of the blessing of the priestly class. He had probably heard the blessing from the lips of priests in temples and synagogues since his childhood. It was the medium God used to communicate his loving favor to his people.

"The Lord said to Moses, 'Say to Aaron and his sons, Thus you shall bless the people of Israel: you shall say to them,/The Lord bless and keep you:/The Lord make his face to shine/upon you, and be gracious to you:/The Lord lift up his countenance/upon you, and give you peace'" (Num. 6:22-26).

The Old Testament took the spoken word seriously. Speech was never idle, passing the day, chitchat. Words were expressions of the will and soul and carried the whole weight of the personality. Thought, word, and deed were seen as one process. If the spoken word were charged with personal power, it was but natural to regard it as having been done. You may recall the familiar words of Isaiah 55:11, "So shall my word be that goes forth from my mouth;/it shall not return to me empty,/but it shall accomplish that which I purpose."

A grace blessing actually imparted the grace of God. A word once spoken had the power to do that for which it was intended. A blessing pronounced by one person for another person was received as a divine blessing. Such was the case in Jacob's blessing of Joseph's sons in Genesis 48:8-16.

The blessing brought the father's inheritance. When Isaac blessed Jacob, he was saying, "All that is mine is now yours." The uttered word could not be revoked. The blessing that should have been given to Esau remained with Jacob. And Isaac had only one blessing to give. All other sons (and daughters) went unblessed.

Jesus brought the good news that the blessing was for everyone. Jesus came blessing everybody—men, women, children, publicans, and sinners. All the Esaus of the world, listen! All that the Father has is now yours. Grace to you!

Grace to you carried on into the New Testament world the Old Testament concept of blessing. Blessing conveyed a gift to another by a powerful utterance. This spoken word was imparted by a person who was a representative of God. This divine favor might be directed to humanity (Gen. 1:28); to another person (Gen. 24:60; 27:4; 48:15); to a land (Heb. 6:7); and as an active response to evil (1 Pet. 3:9).

The Language of Communication. Grace to you is the language of Christian communication. It is the way we say hello and good-bye. It is both a physical and a verbal act. We say it by knowing people's names; by looking them in the eyes; by a touch on the head, shoulders, or arms. In the Bible, the blessing was often preceded by the uplifting of hands to heaven and bringing the blessing down upon a person, as if holding it in your hand and pouring it out over a person's body.

Grace to you is the beginning and ending of all Christian interpersonal relationships. Because God accepts you, I accept you. Acceptance is unqualified and unconditional. When we stand together in the light of God's loving favor, we don't have to say anything, prove anything, defend anything. There is room for freedom and error. There is the power to hear and be heard. Grace holds it all together. Grace carries the beat.

In a group, *grace to you* means the free expression of ideas, attitudes, and opinions without fear of judgment or intimidation. *Grace to you* means that I give you full attention when you speak, knowing and appreciating the fact that what you say has value. *Grace to you* is the power behind the group tools and techniques that make for good discussion.

In his travels across the Mediterranean world, Paul heard many greetings. The Roman greeting was "health to you." The Greek uttered as his best wish, "Joy to you." The Hebrew emphasis *shalom* brought "peace to you." But a new greeting was coined by the Christians bringing forward the rich Hebrew heritage of blessing and emphasizing the free, unmerited favor of God through his Son, Jesus Christ: grace to you.

Christ as Source of the Personal (1:1)

God as "Father" and the "Lord Jesus Christ" appear twice in the first three verses. It is "in" them and "from" them that the interpersonal takes place. Christ is an open flower to the warmth of the Father's love. Because they are personal, we can be personal with one another. This distinguishes our relationships from those outside the faith. We live "in" Christ day by day. Because we are in him, we find ourselves closely related to one another. Throughout this letter, Paul closely associated the Father and the Son (1:3; 2:14; 3:11-13; 5:18,23). In this sphere of relationship, the personal takes on its complete meaning.

Who You Are to Me (1:2-4)

We never can get some people out of our minds and hearts. They keep popping into our thoughts at all times of day and night. In some ways, they are attached to our deepest yearnings and aspirations. They become part of us. When their images persistently invade our waking and sleeping moments, we find ourselves talking about them. We might call them, or we might sit down and write them letters. That's what Paul did in writing to the Thessalonians.

Paul began a style of writing here that continued throughout the letter, addressing them with strong affirmations of friendship and commitment. A quick review of chapter 1 shows the strength of his declarations of affirmation and gratitude.

"We give thanks to God always for you all" (1:2).

"Remembering . . . your work . . . love . . . hope" (1:3).

"He has chosen you" (1:4).

"You became an example" (1:7).

"The word of the Lord sounded forth from you" (1:8).

"Your faith in God has gone forth everywhere" (1:8).

You All (1:2)

Apparently Paul knew each member personally. He remembered them distinctly, not as a group but one by one. There is always risk in telling people what they mean to us. We immediately become vulnerable, opening ourselves to misunderstanding as well as deepening relationships. But Paul did not hesitate. He said, "I remember you all." This is an emphatic "all" in the Greek. He did not group them all together with a southern "y'all" but called them all by name. Paul was able to give thanks for all of them. There were no exceptions. It is easy to give thanks for people who please us. It is not easy to give thanks for people who disturb us. Paul was able to give thanks for all.

Calling Your Names in Prayer (1:2)

How is it possible to remember each one without exception? The secret is in calling their names in prayer. This is the power of praying for others. As we pray, the Lord brings others to our minds. Prayer is an exercise in community, binding people together corporately as well as focusing on each one separately. The problem with prayer is vagueness. Since prayer is a language of love, it has more power as it becomes more specific. We don't pray for all the people until we pray for specific people. In remembering people in prayer, we "member" them in our thoughts and feelings. Paul said we are "constantly mentioning [each one of] you in our prayers."

This remembering seems to have been an occasion that was regularly repeated. He was always doing it or constantly doing it. He encircled them with his thoughts and his prayers—every one of them and the church as a whole. He used the word "remembering" in Ephesians 1:16 and in Romans 1:9, "I mention you always."

Apparently Paul, Timothy, and Silvanus had times of prayer. "At our times of prayer" would be the most accurate picture of what was happening. The Thessalonians were "all" mentioned in prayer because their names were verbalized, spoken out loud so that others could hear. The sound barrier of prayer is broken through personal verbalized accounts.

Remembering You (1:3)

I find significant people like these in my own experience through memory. Sometimes they appear in the twilight zone of dreams. They are hazy figures at first, but quickly they become sharper and closer to reality. I suddenly awake at 3:00 in the morning with them on my mind. Their lives are before me as if I were on a magic carpet, looking over them. Their dilemmas, hopes, work patterns, and life-styles become part of that hazy land between sleeping and waking.

My hunch is that these experiences introduce deeper relationships between people. Relationships remain insignificant until others "come to mind" and we have moments of reflections about our common experiences. When that begins to happen, I want to say, "I thought about you last night," or "You came to my mind yesterday." But often I hesitate, too embarrassed or too afraid to move the relationship to a new level. For when I call a name in the depths of my own being, I am saying that that person has become a part of me.

Some of these memories are painful. They cripple our ability to relate adequately to present situations. But the recalling of the past has a way of sensitizing us to life struggles. The healing of memories happens when we discover that painful moments of our pasts need no longer cripple us.

These moments become gifts to us. The memory of any event can either bless or cripple.

I am recalling the note from a friend that said, "I am trying to erase this event from my mind." Erasing memories is impossible. It is impossible to forget something by our own efforts. Memories, good or bad, cannot be removed as if they were pieces of furniture in a house. Our memories are not forgotten; they are healed. They are incorporated into our lives by our ability to reflect on them and learn from them. The way to achieve skill in forgetting, if you do want to forget, is not by practicing the art of forgetting. There is no art of forgetting. Memories are healed by practicing the art of learning.

Through memory, the past becomes alive and full of meaning. It is impossible to change the past, except as we reinterpret and learn from it. To remember is to call into present awareness some past events or relationships which bestow meaning to our present situations. When I ask you "What do you remember?" I am asking something about who you are, what you value, and how and why you love. The Hebrews viewed memory as an act of the heart, traveling to the deepest levels of being. When people say "I remember," they are saying something important about themselves.

What did Paul remember? What he remembered brought meaning to his life. For the most part his memories were good. He said that he was bearing in mind continually their work of faith, their labor of love, and their steadfastness of hope.

This is the first time that this trio of virtues appears in the New Testament. Paul developed these by observing the ministry of the Thessalonians, not through an abstract statement of belief. We have them again in 1 Thessalonians 5:8 and in Colossians 1:4 and in a different order in 1 Corinthians 13:13. Note how he stated them: Faith works, love toils, and hope endures. This same combination of work, toil, and endurance is descriptive of the church in Ephesus in Revelation 2:2.

Your Faith Works. The word for *work* (*ergon*) is a term meaning business, employment, or task. It implies that faith is our business, our task, our vocation. Paul sharply combined these two words like two flints striking against each other. We are justified by faith, but faith produces work. Jesus taught it, John the Baptist taught it, Paul taught it, and James taught it. Paul never put the two together more closely than he did here. He remembered that the faith of the Thessalonians was a working faith.

Good faith is strong, energetic, and vital. Jesus taught the power of faith. His promises are conditioned with "if you have faith." Paul may be saying here, "If you do not work your faith is flacid, sick, close to death."

Your Love Toils. What a striking statement for Paul to make. He remembered that their love toiled. The word *toil* is not to be restricted to manual labor, although that is part of it. Rather it implies a persistent energy that gradually wears one out. This labor of love brought a glowing goodwill to others. But in reality, it was a strenuous, sweating kind of effort. Paul was saying, "Your love has meant much hard work."

Toiling love does not calculate the worth of the one who is loved or the return that might come from loving a person. Love is freely given, no strings attached. In some way, it must be manifested through daily living. It knows no limits and goes beyond what was expected. Persons committed to love never let disappointments overtake them. They labor at love until exhausted and then go on some more. Loving is a perpetual demand. But when we are into it, we discover that we can do far more than we ever expected. Paul was saying, "Love sweats it out."

Church work is work! When you get involved in the life of a church, it will consume you. It will demand the best of your energies and skills. It will take boundless reservoirs of enthusiasm and energy. The words *labor of love* reveal the nature of ministry. It is a ministry of hard work, exertion, and endurance. This is the secret of a vital church. The people find glory in toiling love.

What is this labor of love? Worship, nurturing the children, equipping the saints are included. Caring for the sick, comforting the dying, instructing those new in the faith are also part of a love ministry.

However, as we look to verses 6-10, it seems that Paul was thinking specifically of communicating the good news and doing this even in the midst of bitter resistance. It was this work of communication that Paul was talking about resulting from strong faith and prompted by radical love.

Your Hope Endures. Endurance is strengthened by hope. Christian love hopes all things and endures all things. Paul was already impressed with this necessary connection between the Christian life and persecution.

Long-distance running has taught me much about endurance. Staying power comes with the ability to tolerate discomfort for extended periods of time. Endurance is not there if it is not practiced. But the capacities for it are almost limitless for those who are willing. Endurance acts as catalyst to bring joy to our present situations. Out of endurance comes hope; hope transforms the present, not the future. The trials, pain, struggles, temptations, and defeats are all transformed by hope.

Paul's message is clear. Etched in his memory was the continuing and fatiguing work of communicating the gospel. Perhaps more than any other kind of work, the practice of interpersonal communication demands much energy, brings on fatigue and emotional depletion, and calls forth a strong endurance and a steadfast patience.

Affirmations (1:4)

Paul closed these expressions of thanksgiving with these strong affirmations.

"*Brothers*" (or "brethren") is a favorite word for Paul in this letter, used some 20 times. The word *brothers* frequently referred to those who were closely associated in some activity. It is the same term used by Jesus in Matthew 23:8. Luke 6:1-3 points to the presence of women in the "brotherhood." I will show later that women were very much a part of Paul's strong affection (see Acts 17), and the term *brothers* for Paul probably incorporated both brothers and sisters.

The ancient world had many male-only groups, such as are characteristic of many contemporary clubs, lodges, and fraternities. But these brothers were different. They were brothers because they were beloved by God and were chosen by him. Therefore, all were included, even if they were sisters! These beloved brothers included a heterogeneous fellowship of Jews, Greeks, Romans, men and women from all economic sections of life.

"*Beloved by God*" is a unique expression found only here in the New Testament. A similar expression "beloved by the Lord" is found in 2 Thessalonians 2:13 and was spoken of Benjamin by Moses in Deuteronomy

33:12. Paul was not satisfied with the mere use of *brothers* here but added another affectionate phrase.

Chosen of God. "Chosen" is the same word Jesus used when speaking of the twelve disciples. "You did not choose me, but I chose you" (John 15:16). Paul undertook no theological explanation of the meaning of election, so the Thessalonians must have understood the concept. Paul was constantly amazed that God had chosen him, so it came as no surprise that God had also chosen the Thessalonians. "God can single you out," he was telling them. He knew from experience and conviction that the Thessalonians had been chosen by God. This tiny little band of Christian witnesses were found in their pagan city because God had chosen them.

Paul was not picky in choosing his friends. His relationships were not built on personal preferences but on the activity of God. These were God's people, brothers and sisters in the faith, beloved of God and chosen by God. God's people will also be our people.

The Power of the Spoken Word (1:5-10)

When Paul came to Thessalonica, his arrival was one of the hinges on the door of Christian history. Thessalonica had been an important city for a long time. At one time, it almost became the capital of the world. It narrowly lost out to Constantinople.

When walking down main street in Thessalonica, a person was walking down the Egnatian Way, the road that linked Rome with the East. Main street, Thessalonica, connected the East with the West as far as the spread of the Christian faith was concerned. For as it spread to the East, it would move into all of Asia; and as it moved West, it would storm even the city of Rome. The communication of faith in Thessalonica was, in a sense, communication to the whole world. If the communication principles worked there, the seed of faith were planted at the very heart of the Roman Empire.

Thessalonica was a large city with a harbor. Picture in your mind the cities of Savannah, Georgia; Mobile, Alabama; and Newport News, Virginia, and you will begin to get the size of Thessalonica. Then place in one of those cities one small church made up of newborn Christians who are being taught the faith for the first time. You have a simple model of interpersonal life. This life was established and nourished by the power of the spoken word.

Word Is Empowered Like Dynamite (1:5)

First, the gospel "came . . . in power." Communicating the gospel had not been "only in word." Words alone are inadequate vehicles. A vital force bigger than words was in operation. The word for power is *dunamis* from which we get our word *dynamite*. It is not simply that the gospel tells of power. When the gospel is taught, God is there working. The gospel *is* power.

Behind the words were persuasion and penetration. Paul delighted in contrasting the mere use of words and the power of the joyful news (1 Cor. 1:18; 2:1-4). God is at work in the communication. That's the difference.

How did Paul know that God was at work? He saw a difference in the Thessalonians' manner of life. More often than to any other people, Paul appealed to their experience (2:1,2,5,11; 3:3,4; 4:2; 5:2). "You know," he said. "In the Holy Spirit and with full conviction" means that God is on the spot beside his people, getting inside them. All creative communication has this emotional quality.

Churches without that power of the Holy Spirit are easy to describe. They are serious but not excited, conventional but not adventurous, decent but not ardent, warm but not burning, casually committed but not possessed. They are a different breed from those filled with power and conviction. Jeremiah found the burden of his message almost greater than he could bear. "There is in my heart as it were a burning fire shut up in my bones" (Jer. 20:9). Amos came down from the hills of Tekoa, yelling indignations. Isaiah's message warmed the heart. John was a burning and a shining light. Apollos preached "fervent in spirit" (Acts 18:25).

Paul's teaching was passionate. In that little church of fervor and passion, the hearts of the members were on fire. Their faith excited them. The wonder of the Lord so possessed them that it showed in their eyes and vibrated in their voices. They were an excited, adventurous, and ardent bunch of people.

Word Leaves Imprint—Stamped Like a Coin (1:6-7)

Second, the teaching of the gospel was characterized by modeling and imitation. The experiences did not rest solely in the teachers. There had been dramatic changes in the lives of the new Christians. Paul said that the Thessalonians were imitators "of us and of the Lord" (1 Thess. 1:6). The learning is often done in that order. We begin by imitating a teacher and then go on to imitate the Master Teacher. If Christians imitate their teachers, it is so that they may be brought to imitate Christ more closely. All this Jesus said very simply. "A disciple . . . when he is fully taught will be like his teacher" (Luke 6:40).

The fact is, we're all going to imitate. We can't help imitating. Why fight it? As children we learn to imitate, and throughout life we're going to imitate. So we should make our imitations consciously purposeful and try to imitate that which is good. Imitation is one of the basic interpersonal principles of the New Testament (1 Cor. 4:16; 11:1; Eph. 5:1; 1 Thess. 2:14; Heb. 6:12; 3 John 11).

A significant change had become evident in the church. That change consisted of the people becoming imitators. The Greek word is *mimetai* from which we get our word *mimic*. They did not simply become followers in the sense of agreeing with their teachers. Rather, as believers in the message, they began to pattern their lives after the examples set by the teachers. It was imitation in a deeper sense of bringing to expression in their own lives something they had seen and detected in others. Imitation was capturing something they had witnessed in others and making it part of themselves.

The teachers were conscious of the new power they had. It showed in the transformation of attitudes, deeds, and speech. They believed that Christ dwelt in them in such a way that others felt compelled to follow them. Because of that power, Paul said, "You people started to copy us and the Lord." Now these young Christians were examples to others.

The message was not only perceived, it was welcomed. The word "received" (1:6) points to a voluntary and willing act. There was no manipulation—getting others to do something they didn't want to do.

The same word is used of receiving or welcoming guests (Luke 10:8,10; Heb. 11:31). We will run into this same word again in 2:13. Receiving the word was seen as an act of faith. It entered their hearts as well as their ears.

The imitators of Paul were in turn imitated by others. He said of these Christians that they were examples (1 Thess. 1:7). Here is another Greek word to remember. His word for "example" is *tupos* from which we get our word *type*. It has the meaning of an image, a model, or a pattern of life (Phil. 3:17; 1 Pet. 5:3). Originally it denoted the mark left by a blow. There is an example of this in John 20:25, where it is translated "print." It came to be used of a figure stamped by a blow, like the design stamped on a coin.

Paul was saying that this church was a pattern community. It was an example for others to follow. It was truly a model church, and it gives us an insight into teaching by example. By following the example of other Christians, we are able to develop into our own worthy and attractive examples for others. Such an achievement is not a matter of length of life but the outcome of a vital inner experience that makes us Christlike.

The words give clear witness to the powerful impact of the Thessalonian church. This was no ordinary church. It had a reputation as a model. Paul described no other church in this way.

They were examples "to all that believe" (KJV). That's even more difficult. It's one thing to be an example to a pagan world; it's another thing to be examples to other believers. The example was backed with their struggles and suffering for the sake of the gospel.

Word Sounds Forth Like a Trumpet (1:8)

The Thessalonians were good examples of interpersonal communication because they spoke clearly. Paul said they were examples to Christians in Macedonia and Achaia. Then he went on to speak of the way the word had gone out from them into every place. And not only did it go out—it went out with power and authority. This reflects something of the strategic situation of Thessalonica. The church was on a great highway running through the middle of town, with a harbor giving ready access to many places. From that highway and harbor came the word of God sounding forth like a trumpet!

"Sounding out" are words found only here in the New Testament. A word of the same root is used in speaking of the roaring of the sea (Luke 21:25) and of the "reports" that went forth about Jesus "into every place in the surrounding region" (Luke 4:37). Hebrews 12:19 uses it to designate the "sound of a trumpet." The meaning of the word is clear. Paul was thinking of the penetration of this church's message and spirit to its community and beyond. No geographical, racial, or cultural barriers could hold it back. In 2 Thessalonians 3:1 Paul asked for the prayers of the Thessalonian Christians "that the word of the Lord may speed on and triumph."

The Thessalonians were under the pressure of persecution. Common sense told them to try to escape notice and avoid danger, to hide as much as possible and keep quiet. But their teaching sounded forth like a trumpet and came crashing in on people like a roll of thunder.

Our word echo comes closest to the Greek word for "sounding out." Paul may have been calling the Thessalonians sounding boards, which reinforce sounds and cause them to travel in various directions. The sounding board does not of itself create the sounds. It occupies a middle position, receiving sounds, reinforcing them, and sending them on. The word of the Lord, having been received, had been reinforced by the Thessalonians' own joyful experience of accepting it. Since it had received new power, it echoed forth, "not only in Macedonia and Achaia, but also in every place" (KJV).

A church knows that its message is being heard when it comes back to them. An echo is a sound we hear after it is reflected (bounced back) from some object. An echo is a sound we hear for a second time. New people are echoes of a church's ministry. When people respond in faith, we know that the message is clear and forceful enough to be heard.

The secret to this church was in the winsome way they developed a warm, spontaneous quality. Their faith was not stiff and unnatural; it was easy and unlabored. They worked at their faith, but they did not perceive it as work! The light showed through them to the pagan world. They were joyful and radiant because of their intimacy with the living Christ. They caught the fire from one another. It is no secret that we grow like those with whom we live. If we live closely to Christ and to other believers, we too will be examples to all the believers. This was said only of the Thessalonian church.

Word Separates and Binds (1:9-10)

The word is loose in the world and has a power of its own. It leaves them and comes back to them. Paul received a report from his own work. All the regions that had been penetrated by the Thessalonian witness gave back a clear signal that the word had been effective. How had it been effective? The word demonstrated its power by dividing them from their past (turning from idols) and by bringing them together into a new future (serving a living God and waiting for his Son from heaven).

The word always serves these two purposes. It separates us, cuts us loose from things to which we might otherwise cling. At the same time, it attaches us, brings us into new relationships, and binds us. It is literally a two-edged sword—separating and dividing, binding and bringing together.

Paul further described these forces at work in three powerful words that express specific changes in behavior—turning, serving, and waiting.

Turning (1:9). The Greek word for *turning* denotes leaving something and clinging to something. The Thessalonians turned "to" God "from" idols. The inner change in their hearts was outwardly expressed in active lives that were moving in a different direction. That is the meaning of transformation and is the goal of turning—to change behavior in a relatively permanent sort of way. Turning is characteristic of transformation. This kind of learning involves the mind, will, and emotion and finds expression in outward conduct.

What we have here is religious revolution—a decisive break with the past and the formation of a radically new life-style. They were throwing out all the things (idols) that had been valued since childhood and were counting them as nothing. Truly, the power of the word had "turned the world upside down" (Acts 17:6).

Serving (1:9). What is the evidence of this radical new life-style? What behavior turns the world upside down? Paul answered these questions in the phrase "to serve a living and true God." The new life-style that flip-flops the world's values is servanthood.

To serve means to serve as a slave. Formerly the Thessalonians had been the slaves of idols. Now they were the slaves of God. They served God who is living and active in contrast to serving dead idols. They served God who is true (genuine) in contrast to idols that were shadowy and counterfeit.

Waiting (1:10). This "turning" and "serving" brings with it a "waiting." This is the only time this (Greek) word is found in the New Testament. From the heavens Jesus will come to bring together his people. This coming they are awaiting with patience and confidence. The word implies being ready for his return. When we wait for visitors to come to our homes, we have prepared all things in advance. Everything is arranged to make the visitors feel perfectly at home with us. The house is in order. We await with anticipation and excitement. It is interesting to note that every chapter of 1 Thessalonians ends with the presence of Christ among his people (1:9-10; 2:19-20; 3:13; 4:17-18; 5:23-24). His presence sums up and completes everything that is personal.

2
The Styles of
Interpersonal Communication
2:1-16

Stoicism was popular in cities like Thessalonica. The Stoics considered feeling to be a weakness. Better to be apathetic than to be influenced by feeling! A strong person was one who tried to reach a stage where he could say to anything: "It doesn't matter. I don't care." Teachers of Stoicism might have said: "Begin with a valued possession. If you break it or tear it, say, 'I don't care.' Go on to a favorite pet or other animal. If it is hurt or killed, say, 'I don't care.' Go on to your own illness. If you break your leg or arm, say, 'I don't care.' Finally, you'll come to a state when you can see your child suffer or your wife die and say, 'I don't care.' Save yourself from disappointment. Do not love people because that will bring suffering. Simply accept things as they are, and you will be happy." The Stoics urged people to lock away every trace of feeling from their hearts. They tried to make the human heart a desolate land and then call it a place of security and peace.

In contrast to this religious philosophy, the teaching of the early church was an overflow of caring and sharing. Paul wanted to make clear the principles of good communication. In chapter 2, he described in great detail the different patterns of communication. Relationships are built around significant personal encounters (2:1-2). He described the faulty methods of communication in 2:3-6. He contrasted these with the healing powers of communication in 2:7-12. Finally, the word of God does its "work" (2:13), in spite of everything (2:14-16).

Significant Relationships Are Costly (2:1-2)

Full, Not Empty (2:1)

Significant relationships are full of meaning. What makes relation-

45

ships significant? Relationships are important because they are demanding. They cost us something. The word for *empty* means empty-handed. The same word is found in Mark 12:3, "They took him and beat him, and sent him away empty-handed." Paul was saying, "When we came to you, our hands were not empty." This harmonizes with 1 Thessalonians 2:8 where Paul is seen as a two-handed giver, both hands full with the gospel and his own life.

The problem is not that many relationships are fruitless. Relationships can be fruitful and still be hollow, lacking in meaning. In 1 Corinthians 15:14, Paul said that hollow preaching leads to emptiness and fruitless faith. We might say the same for our relationships—hollow relationships lead to empty faith. Paul described both empty and full relationships.

Any kind of relationship is better than relationships described by emptiness. Erik Erikson's description of the development of basic trust places heavy importance on the fact that an infant must perceive relationships to have meaning at a basic level. This forms the basis for a sense of being "all right," of being oneself, and of becoming what other people trust one will become. Parents must be able to represent to the child a deep, almost "bodily" conviction that there is meaning in what they are doing. Better to have meaning through pain and struggle than to face the void of emptiness. When we lack the assurance that relationships are meaningful, we are faced with the overpowering anxiety that life is ultimately pointless. Relationships that are filled with turmoil and conflict are more tolerable than relationships that mean nothing. Relationships that lack meaning lead people to a sense of despair.

Boldness in Spite of Pain and Conflict (2:2)

Paul related to the Thessalonians out of deep hurt. The Greek word for *boldness* comes from two words describing a state of mind where words flow freely with no sense of inner blockage. This includes a freedom from fear about what people will think and a sense of complete confidence that what is said will be accepted and understood. However, for Paul, this freedom of expression came in the midst of much opposition. The word *conflict* is a descriptive one. It comes from the athletic world, meaning a contest or race. From this word we get our word *agony*. This possibly refers both to physical and outward conflict (Phil. 1:30) and mental agony or inward striving (Col. 2:1). In 1 Timothy 6:12 and 2 Timothy 4:7, the word describes fighting "the good fight."

I'm sure that Paul would not know what to do with our emphasis on the alleviation of stress. Of course, there is good stress and bad stress. The fact is, the gospel will create stress. The Christian's response to stress is not to alleviate it but to build a higher endurance to it.

Living Tricky: Patterns of Deceptive Communication (2:3-6)

Paul began with a description of his appeal or exhortation. He described his style of communication, what it was and what it was not. Exhortation literally means "to speak out helpfully." The same idea is found in Hebrews 10:24: "Let us consider how to stir up one another to love and good works." Exhortation convicts, encourages, and comforts people through stirring speech. But it is not "tricky" speech. Paul painted this contrast in sharp colors.

Deception (2:3)

Paul said that his exhortation was not made in deceit (error) or in uncleanness or in guile. He was saying that his appeal did not spring from error. He was not trying to delude people. In other words, he did not lie to them.

The second accusation, "uncleanness," carried the connotation of moral impurity. Paul was referring specifically to communication that is sensual in nature and has the purpose of seduction. It is true that sensuality and seduction are means of communication. The sensuality of religion in Paul's time was rampant, and the ritual of prostitution was carried on in connection with many temples. The Jews frequently brought these accusations of immorality against the Christians.

The third accusation is that of using trickery. The word translated *guile* originally had reference to catching fish by means of bait. Guile is a crafty design for deceiving and catching people who are unaware and vulnerable. Honest communication never leaves persons feeling that they are about to be had.

In these verses Paul described the life-style of deception. The skills of deception are trickery and delusion. The style of deception is an ability to live at the expense of other people.

How do people pull off lives of deception? They simply become masters of distorting appearances. If deception becomes visible, it immediately loses its power. Therefore, a great deal of energy is spent on "seeming." There is a semblance of genuineness from all outward indications. We think we are perceiving an honest person.

I remember listening for an hour to a woman selling computer learning centers. She was truly a professional communicator, every word phrased accurately and distinctly. Every gesture was appropriate to the occasion. I could see that others were impressed. But after listening to her for fifteen minutes, I began to get uncomfortable. And then I knew. She was an extension of her product. Her affect never changed. Just plug her in, and she went through the motions as if some invisible powers were programming her every word and movement. She had mastered the power of appearance—a highly controlled person operating a highly controlled computer. She had learned all the mechanics of communication without the heart to go with it. She and machine were one!

Paul said that his appeal to the Thessalonians was not deceptive. It did not come from delusion or from impurity or with a purpose to deceive. Implied in these words are many of the tools of tricky communication—lying, seduction, taking advantage of real spiritual excitement, and juggling the facts to fit the occasion.

What causes a person to develop a life of trickery? The Bible describes the basic evil in the hearts of persons that leads to lives of deceit and treachery. That evil is greed, an insatiable desire to have more, a compulsion to accumulate "stuff." This "itch" can never be satisfied. It encourages people not only to acquire what they sensibly need but also to grab all they can. It shows itself in "more" income, a "choice" home, an "exclusive" vacation, an "elite" education, and "a superior" job. This insatiable drive is usually shrugged off as inconsequential with a simple, "Everyone likes to have nice things" or "I owe it to myself and my family." That's where it becomes tricky. For on the surface, it appears to be a harmless fancy. But at the heart, it is a snare and a trap which lead a person to move everything toward his or her own interest and advantage.

False Approval (2:4)

Over against these points, Paul stated that he was not a trickster. He was aiming at pleasing God and not people. He was putting his communication to the test. The test comes not from people but from God who is always searching out the whole of our inner lives. Paul might have served people, but he was not serving them with the aim of simply pleasing them. He was concerned with service that would be well pleasing to God.

Flattery and Greediness (2:5)

Paul then turned to some other characteristics of tricky communication. First, he dealt with "words of flattery." Flattery is a use of acceptable speech for the purpose of lulling another into a sense of security so that one can obtain one's own ends. Flattery does not simply mean complimentary words intended to tickle the ears. It is rather the smooth-tongued orator who aims at making a favorable impression to gain influence over others for selfish advantage. It carries with it the meaning of guile and cajolery. *Cajolery* comes from a word meaning the chatter of a bird in a cage. At the center of it is a means of persuading another to do one's own will. Flattery is always deceptive because it bombards us with soothing words and false promises. The Greek word for *flattery* is found nowhere else in the New Testament.

The second charge contains the idea of insincerity. The term "cloak" denotes a pretext which conceals the real motive. The cloak implies a hidden agenda. It is a cover for the lust of covetousness. Colossians 3:5 says that covetousness must be put to death because it is idolatry. The greed that cannot be satisfied leads to a dishonesty in every area of life and cruelties of every shape and form. First Thessalonians 2:5 describes this deceptive appearance as "a cloak for greed." For who would boast of being greedy? The Bible says that, though many are greedy, they will try to hide it with a handsome cloak.

The cloak of respectability often covers the life of cheating. It shows itself in limited demands and the narrow range of interests that are related to one's personal needs and the immediate needs of family and close friends. There is no desire to be overly good, rather the objective is to deflect the appearance of evil.

Someone has said the one defect in the making of persons is that there are no windows to the inner life. The honest person is transparent. He or she, by choice, opens windows to words and actions so that the innermost thoughts and intentions are visible and apparent. Proverbs 14:7-8 says it well: "Avoid a stupid man,/you will hear not a word of sense from him./A clever man has the wit to find the right way;/the folly of stupid men misleads them./A fool is too arrogant to make amends;/upright men know what reconciliation means" (NEB).

Paul said, in effect: "Beware of the flashy people with lots of style and little substance. On the surface the teaching may look good and sound good, but beneath it is a selfish motive covered with the cloak of greediness."

Words can be used to do anything the speaker wants—to make contact, to state facts, to invoke anger, to distort, to charm, or to seduce. Words can be used to confuse. Then more words must be added to cover up words. The flood of verbiage can drown us in meaningless words. Communication is meant to flow like a clear stream, to provide sparkle and joy and refreshment. But Paul said that words are often used to muddy the waters. They can poison relationships and can stagnate the flow of meaningful human interaction.

Seeking Glory (2:6)

In back of tricky talk is the need for glory. "Glory" stands for the expression of esteem or praise. Paul was saying that people use deceptive communication to find ways of esteeming themselves. Praise is a heady tonic. For those who need it, there is never enough.

Good Communication: "Too Much for Words" (2:7-12)

As a Mother Nurses Her Children (2:7)

Then, what is good communication? The best model of communication is seen in a mother caring for her children. The image here is of a mother nursing her child. The mother caresses her children, comes down to their level, uses their language, and plays their games. Paul likened himself to a mother who nurses, caresses, and cherishes her children. The same word is used in Deuteronomy 22:6 of a mother bird sitting over the young in the nest.

In the deepest experience of human interaction, words often fail. We say that a profound experience is "just too much for words." The study of a mother's and baby's interaction provides us with insight into these beautiful combinations of communication.

Close-up films of mothers and their babies show a common sequence. Without being aware of it, most women cradle the infant in their left arm where the infant can hear and be soothed by the maternal heartbeat. The mother touches the baby's fingers and toes with her own fingertips, puts the palm of her hands on the baby's trunk, and encloses the infant with her arms. Long, drawn-out words that only resemble conversations with other people are heard. All the while there is a movement and adjustment of heads to a face-to-face position to achieve full parallel eye contact. All of this would be perceived as bizarre behavior if it were directed to anyone but an infant. Many women would have difficulty repeating it if they were not looking directly into their babies' faces. But the interpersonal response is so intense, so significant, that all self-consciousness is lost.

I clearly remember observing such events when Lela was nursing our children. They were some of the most profound religious experiences of my life. I was an observer but I did manage to get my arms around both of them. There are few human interactions that can match such beauty and significance. The importance of this early contact cannot be overestimated. Those mothers who are allowed to handle their babies from the earliest moments lay the foundations for religious experience—love, faith, and trust.

This need for mutual recognition through the encounter of responsive faces never ceases. The uplifted face, hopeful of being recognized, brings together persons with God—face-to-face. If this encounter is so vital, why the aversion, the fear of exposure, the embarrassed glances? Why the fear of losing face and suffering shame? Why do we give ourselves away by blushing. Why do we go to any length to avoid an eye-to-eye encounter with another person? The face as the mirror of the soul expresses the depths of personhood.

Erik H. Erikson, in *Young Man Luther*, told of a young mental patient who "drew and painted dozens of women's faces, cracked like broken vases, faded like worn flowers, with hard and ungiving eyes, or with eyes like stars, steely and blinking, far away."[1] Only when the patient painted a healthy and wholesome face did the doctor know that he could be cured.

The mother-and-child model of interpersonal relationships has much to say about religious education. All religious experience of significance must recognize otherness. Experiences may shake us or arouse us to new insights, but they have no powerful spiritual significance unless they hold an unmistakable presence of something other than ourselves.

In the mother-child relationship, there is someone who is close to the mother who is not the mother. A mother may fail to recognize this otherness of her child. She may only see the child as an extension of herself. She may be caught up only in her experience of the child. She may be concerned with what the child makes her feel more than she is struck by what the child is feeling apart from her.

The denial of otherness blocks human communication. The block may occur in two ways. We may see others as extensions of ourselves. Or we may experience others as threatening. Consider the following case study.

A mother was concerned about her irrational outbursts of hatred toward her children. She found herself exploding in anger at them, anger which was out of all proportion to the incidence and which filled her with resentment at their very presence. After several months of therapy, a very complicated conflict came to life. The mother wanted to suppress her awareness that her children existed in their own right as persons other than herself, entitled to identities separate from herself. To acknowledge her children's otherness, she would have to acknowledge something else: she was different from them. She resisted this self-knowledge because it led to still another acknowledgment: she was other than her own mother. Even in her adult life, this woman felt herself to be essentially an extension of her mother's existence. Realizing her separateness opened up a totally new world of interpersonal life to her.

The Gospel and Our Own Lives (2:8)

Paul's life was intermingled with the Thessalonians. He spoke of being "among you" (2:7). There seems to be the taking of a place of equality. Jesus used the same expression in Luke 22:27, "But I am among you as one who serves." All good communication brings us to the same level of others, which is the essence of sympathy and compassion. Paul was very gentle in the midst of the people, as one of them and not as one apart from them.

In 1 Thessalonians 2:8, Paul used some of his most intimate conversation. With the affection of a wet nurse (or mother), he was eager "to share not only the gospel of God but also our own selves" because the converts had become very dear to him. Paul said that he "yearned" after them. This word used in the original Greek occurs only here in the New Testament. It expresses a great depth of desire. The translation that Paul was "affectionately desirous of you" brings out this powerful appeal. The words *yearning for* mean to desire, to long for. It implies a deep longing that attaches one to other persons. It denotes strong and intense affection.

Paul was no detached communicator of truth. His life's blood was mixed with his teachings. It has been said that the medieval painters mixed their own blood with their paints in order to get "their own selves" into the canvas. The thought of giving oneself is the very essence of all genuine Christian teaching. In profound communication, we are not allowed to keep our innermost selves to ourselves. A cool, detached verbalization of content without mixing it with one's own life story is at the root of much ineffective communication. Paul was a two-handed teacher—in one hand, good news (content); in the other hand, his own life (experience).

The opening of our hearts to others is always appropriate in Christian conversation. Communication is a rich mixture of subject matter and personal experience. Paul gave all of himself in these verses. He might have been saying, "Those who slander us are saying that we are out to get you; well, they are right, we were indeed yearning for you, but the purpose was not to take something from you but to share our very own lives with you."

The Gospel and My Life

Two strong recurring themes in 1 Thessalonians are love and work. This is our need—a work to do and a people to love. Many of our failures come from the lack of loving. Somewhere, sometime, in the midst of our working we must catch up on our loving.

When I was in my late twenties, working and loving came to a standstill. I was well acquainted with work, having worked most days since my fourteenth birthday. I thought I knew about love; but in reality, I knew very little. In the midst of an active and productive life came a lull, a hesitation, an inner reminder that something had been forgotten. I could not move on until I retraced my steps and found it.

If I had known then what I know now, I would have sought a moratorium, a span of time to go back and pick up what had been lost, a postponing of the decision of who I was and what I wanted to be. In Erik Erikson's words, there was a dawning realization that I was becoming fatally overcommitted to what I was not. Somewhere there was a "road less traveled" which could not be quickly journeyed but only slowly walked through, one painful step at a time.

But I did not know. So I wandered, not knowing what I was looking for or what I would do if I found it. There was the compelling, almost irresistible impulse to be close to people, lots of people, as if the number of people could somehow fill the void of significant contact. And if I could find closeness in numbers, I could avoid the frightening possibility of being close to a few.

This is the vicious cycle of the intimacy dilemma—an alternating force of needing to be close and at the same time rejecting closeness. This is the paradox—a deep inexpressible need for interpersonal warmth, yet living on a plain of shallowness and superficiality in a world full of familiar strangers.

At the same time, I grew fearful that I possessed a fundamental structural flaw somehow different from any other person. Whatever it took, I would have to keep it hidden from those who knew and loved me. Enormous reservoirs of energy were needed to conceal this flaw. I wanted to get on with life; but the path I was traveling was strange, unknown, and dangerous. For the first time, I felt forces at work that I could not control through my own will and effort. The harder I tried to push on, the more the delay took root and grew. The more I needed people who loved me, the more I isolated myself from them. The more information I gathered on human development and communication, the more anxiety tuned up to higher levels. The more desperately I needed some word from the Lord, the more muffled and distant became the still, small voice.

You must understand that my emotional terror came from the inability to verbalize my dilemma. My prayers were emotional "rummagings," simply thoughts running into each other in my mind. I know how difficult it is to verbalize feelings, to "break the sound barrier" with the inner life.

In the midst of this overwhelming anxiety came the night to remember when "grace to you" was heard with the "inner ear" for the first time. Later came the courage to talk to a friend-counselor. After several sessions, he said: "You have the most intense need for emotional intimacy of any person I have ever met. You must learn to meet your need for closeness through talk."

And so it is. To this day, loving is talking. Not just any kind of talking, but intense talking, riveted, face-to-face, up close, without distraction, verbal and nonverbal, "like a [mother] taking care of her children" (2:7). Like an infant, I was learning to talk, first with Lela, then with a friend-counselor, then through the miraculous power of a small group. And finally, I got some biblical perspective on it all in the context of 1 Thessalonians 2:7-8.

Hard Work (2:9)

Good communication is also reinforced through hard work. The Thessalonians' toiling love in 1:3 leads me to believe that manual labor was a definite characteristic of their community. There is a special intimacy in energy-consuming work. People relate well to one another if they are not afraid to get their hands dirty. Paul reminded his readers of this incessant toil. Paul and his companions had worked hard to support themselves so that they would be no burden to others. The word "labor" denotes a work that produces weariness. The word "toil" implies overcoming a great deal of difficulty. This was not token work they were doing. They worked hard, and they worked constantly—"night and day." This was another way that Paul found to live in the midst of the people. It bound them together in a more intimate network. They had placed themselves on the same level with the people of Thessalonica. They all worked for a living! It was part of their spiritual bond.

Again, the themes of love and work are dominant. Nothing builds community like a good mixture of these two dynamics in people. When you find a people committed to love and work, you find a treasure. For there you will find people who love to work and work at loving. The secret to combining these two is dedicating oneself to loving rather than to being loved and to working together rather than needing to achieve or to be successful.

Right Conduct (2:10)

Paul was also able to back his teaching with right conduct. Three adverbs are used to indicate right conduct—*holy, righteous,* and *blameless.* Paul said this "was our behavior to you believers." The three words imply devotion to God, high moral character, and living above reproach. Whatever other people in Thessalonica might have thought of the missionaries, the church members had good opinions toward them. The men backed the message with their lives. Again, Paul was making a point of saying that greedy ambition was not the hidden motivation behind their work.

Like as a Father (2:11)

The other model of communication that Paul used was that of a father with his children. Again, note the very personal dealing that Paul had with the people. "Each one of you" implies attention to individuals. Each one was cared for personally. Paul was both mother and father to them. They received both a mother's affection and tenderness (2:7) and a father's thought and counsel (2:11). He admonished the Corinthians in the same way, "my beloved children," in 1 Corinthians 4:14.

Paul used three words in 2:11 that describe this kind of fatherly communication. First, he said that "we exhorted each one of you." Exhorting is a powerful summons or appeal. It is a word that penetrates with warnings, consolations, and encouragement. The purpose of exhortation is to arouse out of indifference and to overcome the resistance of the will. Here it carries with it a direct and personal force toward quality spiritual living. Exhortation helps people envision, or get a picture of, the persons God wants them to be.

Paul then said, "We . . . encouraged you." Once the goal of maturity is clarified, people need help in taking necessary steps toward growth. Encouragement is needed to help people overcome difficulties. The same word is found elsewhere in the New Testament in 1 Thessalonians 5:14 and John 11:19,31. In 1 Thessalonians 5:14, it expresses encouragement for the fainthearted. In John, it expresses comfort for the bereaved. It implies consolation. The word of encouragement is spoken specifically to those who find difficulty in living the Christian way of life in the face of opposition.

Finally, Paul said, "We . . . charged you." The Greek word used here is difficult to translate. It means to bring forth a witness in strong testimony. It is used this way in Acts 20:26 and in Galatians 5:3. Charging is a solid declaration of truth. It may refer to those serious words addressed to those who have slackened in their faith. The word comes from the Greek word meaning martyr. The same word is used of the "cloud of witnesses" in Hebrews 12:1. It implies expectation and observation. The father is the one who is ready to testify about performance. He watches over with both a loving and critical eye.

Fathering is the difficult task of providing both affectional warmth and challenge. Fathering that promotes high expectations without warmth and instruction often produces children who are ambitious but angry that they are not recognized but unable to be productive enough to gain recognition. Without this balancing side of communication, children often grow up with strong needs to be loved and to please rather than to be competent and strong.

A firm sense of identity comes from finding a work to do and being loved for doing it. This sense of identity is helped along by fathering—a mixture of warmth, instruction, and expectation. The message that comes from fathering is the strong challenge to "do it!" Without this toughness in relationships, the soft side often remains the only side; and we remain childlike and insecure without any kind of direct confrontation. This is true of men and women who lacked fatherly instruction when they were children. Because we are aware of this vulnerability, of this soft and fragile side, we often fail to deal with people with directness and candor.

In summary, communication is both tough and tender. The two always seem to go together. Love is the binding force. Love requires us to respond to the same person tenderly at one time and toughly at another time. There is always a place for the warm, tender response. We must learn to give both.

First Thessalonians 2 gives us an adequate model for basic interpersonal skills. Attending is the first skill—learning to listen, paying close attention to the full context of the conversation, listening to both words and silences, to emotions and ideas, and to the full situation in which the conversation takes place. Attending is the first act of communication. If I cannot pay full attention, it will be difficult for me to listen. If I do not listen, it will be difficult for me to understand accurately and effectively.

Asserting is the other skill. This means presenting our own insights and beliefs forcefully, but without manipulation. It searches out and challenges. It calls for an appreciation of my own experiences, needs, and purposes in such a way that I can state them clearly. It calls forth from me an expression of what I really believe. It demands a skill of concreteness— my ability to be clear and specific in what I want to say.

First Thessalonians 2 presents these two helpful ways of interpersonal relating. Both can be considered to be loving responses. People are assumed to be responsive, friendly, and teachable. So, it is OK to be warm and close. We seek to help, cooperate, and appreciate. But we can also state our position clearly and forcefully. We assert, express, and let be. One style brings forth teaching, parenting, and nurturing. The other style brings forth the forces of challenging, motivating, and exhorting.

But, there is another style. This style expects submissiveness and plays on dependency, weakness, and insecurity. People are assumed to be distrustful, resistant, and skeptical. Therefore, we lead by calculation, deception, appearance, and the "sleight of hand." People can be cajoled, tricked, and flattered. Any price is worth paying as long as we are protected and come out "looking good." This can be called the power response. Anything goes as long as people do what we want them to do.

Walking (2:12)

The end result of the powerful interpersonal communication Paul taught was that the Thessalonians would lead lives (walk) in a manner worthy of (in harmony with) God who keeps on calling them into the future. All of the communication skills and patterns that Paul developed to this point were directed toward seeing the Thessalonians "walk worthy of God" (KJV). Paul was looking forward to seeing certain results in their lives. *Walking* was one of Paul's favorite ways to describe the whole of a person's life. It is a dynamic word, pointing to God's future rule in the lives of men and women as he "calls you into his own kingdom and glory."

How Good Communication Is Received (2:13-16)

The Word of God "Works" (2:13)

First Thessalonians 2:13 describes this church's response to this communication. They did not receive it as a word from a man but as a word from God. There is an interesting contrast between the two words for "received" and "accepted" in this verse. In the first half of the verse, the word for "received" is one which describes an objective outward receiving. The message is heard and understood. The second word, "accepted," describes a joyous welcome. The Thessalonian Christians had not merely heard it with their ears, but they had embraced it and appropriated it in their hearts. It is much the same expression that we find in 1:6. The word was heard, received, welcomed, and was operating in the inner lives of the believers. That word was nothing less than God's own word and not as a word from a man.

The same word is used of receiving guests into our homes. How do we receive guests? Are they received with a certain amount of caution and formality? Or are they received with the open arms of excitement and anticipation? This is the issue of intimacy with the word of God. Paul at least implies that openness to the word is in some way related to our interpersonal openness. When we are able to welcome others into our lives and hearts, we "practice" the attitude that is necessary for God's word to touch us at a deep level.

Paul sees the word of God "at work in you." This phrase is almost always used in the New Testament as some form of God's activity. It says much about how the word of God is communicated and received. From this word we get our word *energy*.

Barclay's *New Testament Words* explores the word *energy* in describing how the word of God does things.

1. The word works like something which is radiant and alive.
2. The word works like a person on duty in his or her profession or calling.
3. The word works like an army which is industrious and fit for active service.
4. The word works like a land which is cultivated and therefore, productive.
5. The word works like a mine which produces minerals.
6. The word works like money and capital which is not lying idle invested in some productive interest.[2]

These images carry meanings of vitality as opposed to deadness, activity as opposed to idleness, efficiency as opposed to uselessness. They describe actions which bring forth results much in the same way that a drug or medicine acts and works in us. One thing is clear, the whole tone shows how the word "works" in effective action. It is not simply action. It is always action which issues in a desired result. In Ephesians 4:16, Paul described the body of the church, harmoniously compounded together according to the "effectual working . . . of every part" (KJV). In the same way, this effective working is the word of God working in the lives of believers in the Thessalonians church. It is the power which has achieved the aim, end, and object which it sets out to achieve.

It is important that we understand the powerful dynamic of the word in transforming our lives. The word goes forth to accomplish a task (Isa.

55:11; Jer. 23:29; 1 Pet. 1:23). Perhaps better than any other passage, Hebrews 4:12-13 describes the dynamic nature of the word. The word of God is living and active. It pierces as far as the division of soul and spirit, through joints and marrow. The word probes and penetrates every aspect of our individual lives and our corporate life. The word illuminates and energizes the inner life. It is able to judge the thoughts and intentions of the heart. The word sifts out and critiques the inner reflections and thinking of the mind and heart. The Scripture pictures how the word touches and transforms the whole person.

In the emotional terror of trying to make my life more transparent to others, I discovered 1 Thessalonians 2:7-8. Rather, this Scripture searched and found me. I had surely heard these words before, but my "faith ears" heard it for the first time. The word came to me through hearing an exegetical sermon on 1 Thessalonians 2:7-8 entitled "Sharing the Gospel and the Self." I remember being amazed that these verses were in the Bible. They spoke so clearly to my dilemma, describing so succinctly my situation.

The impact was not immediate. But a seed had been planted. Several weeks later those phrases "like a [mother] cares for her children" and "sharing the gospel and the self" kept popping into my mind. I tried to find the verses again. All I could remember about 1 Thessalonians was, *It's something about the second coming.* But here was a description of my intimacy dilemma right in the middle of a book on the second coming of Christ! It rattled all my theological nerves. I laughed to myself, *How did Paul know that about me?* The last place I expected to find help was from old, crusty Paul. I pictured Paul as the guy who wrote all that stuff to keep Christians from having any fun!

I'm sure that I had experienced transforming moments with Scripture before, but not with this same intimacy and intensity. These verses stuck in my mind. I could not escape them. I imagined writing books about them, preaching great sermons from this text. As far as I was concerned, I had found the jugular vein of 1 Thessalonians. In fact, it seemed that I had found the key verses to the Bible. For me, life flowed from those two verses.

I'm trying to describe how the Scripture began to do their work. It did not give me answers, mind you. It simply began to ferment in my life. Hebrews 4:12-13 tells my story better than I can. For the first time, the word became "living and active." In the midst of my dilemma, the word found me—singled me out, took me aside—and spoke a personal message to me. It was "sharper than any two-edged sword, piercing to the division of soul and spirit, of joints and marrow" (Heb. 4:12). Suddenly the word was probing around in my life, touching everything, laying it all open, "discerning the thoughts and intentions of the heart." For the first time in my own awareness, the word spoke to my desires, passions, and feelings. For the first time, the masquerade and disguises were "open and laid bare."

The Greek word for *laid bare* is the aggressive word of a wrestler downing his opponent by grabbing him around the throat. As I write these words, I have been watching Jud, my son, compete in junior high school wrestling. He is small, wiry, and quick and, at this time in his life, is tough to beat in his weight class. Wrestling is a fascinating sport. There is the circling of the mat, of stalking and being stalked, of maneuvering and searching for quick advantages. Suddenly the movements become more frantic, the struggles become more desperate, the grips become firmer, and the body is held fast to the point of becoming immovable. There is no way to escape. This is the image of Hebrews 4:13 and the experience of my life. I had been grabbed by the Scripture, wrestled to the floor, and finding no way to escape I had been pinned, "laid bare" by the transforming power of the word.

In Spite of Everything (2:14-16)

These verses further reveal the field of forces that helps and hinders the communication of the gospel. In contrast to the mind that is open to the "working" of the word of God is the mind trapped in tradition and spiritual arrogance. The Jews "who killed both the Lord Jesus and the prophets" thought they pleased God. But, in reality, they "displease God and oppose all men by hindering us" (2:15-16).

The Jews' minds were locked into preconceived patterns. They had all the right answers to all the right questions. More and more they became separated from the common people by talking only among themselves. They used the word on a ten-foot pole to guard, punch, and jab. Whatever needed to be said had already been said and only needed repeating. They—the elite of the professional religious class—knew it all. They were proud, egotistical, haughty, arrogant under the guise of being the Lord's true servants.

We do not have to look for these great hinderers of the gospel among alien lands and people. Rather, they can be found "from your own countrymen" (v. 14). The spiritually arrogant are found all along the theological spectrum. Just as the fresh breezes begin to blow, the "contrary" winds will pick up force. The word *contrary* (KJV) (*oppose*, RSV) in 2:15 refers to winds in Acts 27:4 and Mark 6:48. Paul pictured these contrary winds coming from contrary people. Even though they cannot actually prevent the progress of the gospel, we can be sure that their hindering presence will be evident. But the word will continue to go forth in spite of everything.

3
The Emotional Quality
of Relationships
2:17 to 3:13

Who were these people that gathered in Thessalonica to hear Paul's love letter? It was a composite group—Jews of the synagogue, Greek proselytes, and women. The majority of the converts were Gentiles—God-fearers made up of all kinds of people in the big city. These were common laborers, business leaders, converted prostitutes, citizens and strangers.

Many women were converts in the early Christian church. Women were more emancipated here than in some portions of the Greek world. They became openly friendly to Paul's message. Whether they were proselytes or Gentiles or Jewish wives of Gentiles, they had more freedom in Thessalonica than women did elsewhere, even though not all of them belonged to the higher classes.

Clearly Paul developed a deep attachment to these men and women. He was compelled to leave before he wished and in circumstances which made him fear for the permanence of the work. Earlier in this letter Paul had written "For what is our hope or joy or crown of boasting before our Lord Jesus at his coming? Is it not you? For you are our glory and joy" (2:19-20).

Can we imagine what it would be like to risk what Paul was risking in this very intimate and personal letter? Risk taking is always a scary venture, particularly when we talk about our feelings toward others. There is always the fear of being misunderstood, of being laughed at, of not being taken seriously. How many of us would write a letter of such personal dimensions and ask that it be read before a group of people? Yet, that is what Paul did (1 Thess. 5:27). How many of us would be willing to write an open letter . . .

1. Disclosing the intensity of our feelings toward people in the group?
2. Recalling the impression that people had left with us?
3. Expressing affection toward people in the group?
4. Making a statement that might anger someone else in the group?
5. Expressing problems and conflicts with people in the group?
6. Openly expressing our intentions and wishes toward people in the group?
7. Openly expressing our deepest longings and desires?
8. Suggesting that our letter be read in front of a group of people who would then discuss its contents?
9. Telling people in the group how important they have become to us?
10. Openly admitting that our happiness is dependent on how people in the group feel about us?

This is what Paul did in the middle section of the Thessalonian letter. He made himself openly vulnerable to all kinds of misunderstanding.

Reading "Between the Lines" with Paul: the Emotional Content of Biblical Language (2:17-20)

To see the emotional nature of Paul's writings, we must relate to him as brother, as one of us. He was in touch with his own suffering, his body and his mind close together. Like us, he struggled to put the feelings of his heart into words. Here we see both Paul's weakness and his power, both his feeling of abandonment as well as his feeling of being chosen. We have only hints of the depth of his emotion. But his words are so intimate, so intensely personal that if we had never seen Paul before, we see him now.

These verses are rich with relational words. In fact, the Scriptures are full of them, yet they are often treated lightly. My involvement with 1 Thessalonians has opened an exciting world of biblical studies—the careful examination of the emotional and relational aspects of the biblical material.

Why did Paul use such powerfully ladened, emotional words to describe his relationship with these people? He used the best words he could find to describe the intensity and direction of his affection. He made no apology for his emotions. If he had been speaking, his voice might have trembled and broken. To get at the emotional content of the biblical language, we must see not only the words but also the feelings behind the words. We must read between the lines.

Abandoned (2:17)

Abandoned means literally "having been orphaned." It is a strong word and fastens attention on Paul's sense of desolation and bereavement. He had been "torn away from" those he loved dearly. Paul didn't mind mixing his metaphors. He was "as a [mother] taking care of her children" (2:7) and "father" (2:11). Next he was "bereft of" them. He was searching for a word that best described his mental anguish. Let us not minimize his torment. Paul cried out like an orphaned child who had suddenly lost all those who were dear to him.

There are few of us who do not know the special pain of losing someone. Some bounce back quickly. Others never quite recover, being filled with a mist of memories which becomes a part of every waking moment. Loss washes to the shoreline of our lives every human emotion. Indeed, the feelings we are left with are so complex that we begin to forget the loss and spend more and more time sorting out the feelings. But the sorting out is difficult. All we know is that much of us has been touched and twisted into a special pain. Some experience loss as betrayal by others and failing on their parts. Loss could have been avoided by compassion, or love, or simply better luck. In our grief, we might think that God has deceived us by letting some powerful force take away the important people in our lives.

My own feelings of abandonment came when I was nine years old. My father was struck with a massive cerebral hemorrhage that left him paralyzed and bedfast for the last eighteen years of his life. Not too long after my father came home an invalid, I experienced my initial bouts with asthma, a restricting pressure about living and breathing resulting from a fear that whoever I loved would eventually leave me. This abandonment was not a loss of physical presence. Rather, it was a loss of contact, a feeling that my parents were no longer "with me" as they had been before.

The dynamics of bronchial asthma create an unusual world. Feelings and sensations become more and more intense. Breath is lifesaving. The moment is important. The interpersonal takes on supreme value. The inner world becomes more alive. Sufferers become seemingly, permanently sensitized to how things are "working" in them. So intense was this initial experience of loss in my father's "in-valid-ness" that abandonment was an ever-present threat in all relationships. In fact, I felt there were super-human forces at work to bring it about.

Paul may have felt some of those forces because he longed to return to the Thessalonians again and again, but he said, "Satan hindered us." The more Paul was blocked off from them, the more powerful became the desire to get back with them. Like a stream that grows more furious by the obstacles set against it, affection grows more turbulent by all that which opposes it.

This deep sense of bereavement was experienced even though the separation had been "for a short time." He experienced abandonment even though the separation was only in physical presence—in person, not in heart. There is no way to minimize the multitude of ways that people experience loss. The stages of grief are never experienced in neat fashion.

In language broken with emotion, Paul insisted that they were eager to return to Thessalonica. Can you imagine these words being spoken face-to-face? Many of us would probably have a difficult time expressing the depth of our feelings in words.

Because of this deep feeling, Paul sought for a word that would describe his mental anguish. The cry of the orphaned child came to his mind. Paul made a determined attempt to visit the Thessalonians. The word "endeavored" combines the two ideas of haste and eagerness. Paul did not delay, nor did he put forth a token effort. Rather he used all his strength, "the more eagerly" to see them.

With Great Desire (2:17)

Paul went on. He wanted to see his friends with great desire. This is a surprising word, for it nearly always means *lust* in the New Testament. Here Paul used it in terms of a very strong desire, almost a fierce passion. With great passion, he wanted to see them face-to-face. He was not ashamed to confess the full force of his longings. The word for *desire* is *epithumia* which means an overwhelming desire. It is the same word that Jesus used when he said, "I have earnestly desired to eat this passover with you" (Luke 22:15). It expresses a priority concern dominant over all other concerns.

This desire to see them again had taken possession of him. He was in the grip of it like a person obsessed. This desire could only be satisfied by seeing them face-to-face. In John's second and third letters, he said that his joy would not be complete until he saw his friends face-to-face. (2 John 12; 3 John 14).

Wishing (2:18)

The word "wanting" does not adequately express the feeling Paul wrote of in this verse. Again the word is connected with the feeling rather than the will. *Wishing* better describes the emotional element at work. Whatever had kept Paul away from the Thessalonians had not been his own desire. Notice the emphasis on "I Paul." Since Paul used the plural "we" in most of this letter, the singular becomes more significant when it does occur. Here the intense personal feeling breaks through. He had not simply made one attempt. He was saying, "I have wished over and over and over again."

Why did not Paul return? There is only the simple statement, "Satan hindered us." We have no way of knowing just what Paul had in mind. Perhaps the Thessalonians knew. The important thing to remember here is that Satan is the great hinderer. He often tries to prevent us from making the forgiving, the connecting, the reconciling response. Satan breaks up roads, destroys bridges, and makes the communication impossible. He is the great hinderer of significant relationships. This is what he is doing in Paul's relationship to the Thessalonians. It is Satan's work to throw obstacles into the Christian's way. His roadblocks are made for us to get around and through.

Thessalonians, You Are the Ones (2:19-20)

Paul spoke of the Thessalonians as being his crown. In the Greek, there are two words for the English word *crown*. The one is *diadema*, a royal crown. The other is *stephanos*, the victor's crown in a contest, especially the athlete's crown at the end of the game. *Stephanos* is used in verse 19. The only prize in life that Paul really wanted was to see his converts doing well. The Thessalonians would be his crown when they appeared before the presence of Jesus.

Here is what I think Paul was saying about the Thessalonians: "I have no hope or joy or crown if you are not all these things to me, and it will be you who adorn me when I come into the presence of Christ. If we can glory at all in our lives, it will be because of you. Who else can it be but you? If it is not you, it will be no one! Why should we seek glory from people (2:6)? You are our glory! Thessalonians, you are the ones!"

Most likely Paul never saw these people again, although he may have returned to Thessalonica on his third missionary journey. Even then, the renewal of relationships would have been brief. They became part of his memories—pilgrims and wayfarers along his journey—significant, if only for a moment. His desire for them was an open wound which kept his inner life turbulent and productive. George Bernard Shaw said, "There are two tragedies in life. One is not to get your heart's desire. The other is to get it." Augustine knew that. So did Kierkegaard. So will many of us.

There was little interpersonal fulfillment in Paul's life. That is one reason he seems distant from us. The lack of any sense of completeness in relationships must have formed a special pain. But without this incompleteness, Paul might never have forged the concepts of the body of Christ and the family of faith that are so characteristic of his later writings. Out of this lack of fulfillment may have come a vision of corporate intimacy that he knew would only find complete expression in the return of Christ, "at his coming" (2:19).

Overcoming Loneliness: the Search for Community (3:1-8)

Paul's time in Thessalonica was short, but it was a critical time in the spread of the Thessalonians' Christian faith. If Paul had to settle down in every city and spend months or even years before he could make an impact, his task would have been nearly hopeless. However, if the sparks of faith would catch and would run like wildfire, then there was hope that the whole Roman Empire could be touched. This was one question in Paul's mind.

But something else was going on. Even though his visit to Thessalonica was for the main purpose of spreading the gospel, Paul's life was caught up with people. His feelings became part of his task. We must remember the dominant way people dealt with their feelings in the ancient world. The Stoics taught that everything happened for the best and, therefore, had to be accepted. Whatever will be, will be. If we cannot get what we want, we must train ourselves to want what we get. If a person had feelings, someone else could make one glad or sad, happy or unhappy. Therefore, every person must be responsible for his or her own happiness apart from other people. Many of the current self-help books describe happiness in much the same way. This was not Paul's experience, as recorded in 1 Thessalonians 3. His own sense of well-being was dependent on the response of other people.

Alone in Athens (3:1)

What is the meaning of "we were willing to be left behind at Athens alone" (3:1)? This is probably a carry-over from Paul's feeling of abandonment found in 2:17. Paul's feeling resulted from his affection for the Thessalonians and his anxiety about their growth in faith. It all accumulated into an experience of loneliness.

Loneliness is a pain resulting from loss of contact. It is much like the loneliness of a teenager who is still too young to date and too old to sit in Daddy's lap. There is a sudden loss of connectedness. Loneliness then accumulates many unexpressed hurts and resentments which keep coming to the surface.

Loneliness calls our attention to two deep relationship needs. One need is the sense of attachment which, for most people, is best provided through an intimate relationship with a spouse and a few close friends. The other need is a sense of community which is best provided through a network of people who share common interests and causes. The absence of either of these provisions results in loneliness. Emotional isolation (the absence of attachment) is more acutely painful. Social isolation (the absence of community) brings with it feelings of restlessness, rejection, and boredom.

Being alone and being lonely are different. Many people are comfortable alone. Some people are alone for days and never complain. But loneliness has to do with feelings of loss following a physical separation from familiar and loved places and people. This was Paul's loneliness, keenly expressed. Separation is not experienced just in a physical sense. The vague anxiety of loneliness in an emotional sense is a deeper pain. Paul was experiencing the anxiety of loneliness because he was not sure that the powerful feelings that he experienced toward the Thessalonians were returned to any degree. Did they experience the same anxieties and affections for him that he experienced for them? He suffered because of the uncertain response to his love. Clark Moustakas says, "All love eventually ends in suffering."

There is another kind of loneliness. There is the loneliness of experiencing a different level of awareness. I am not suggesting that this level is more profound. But it is different enough that other people say, "I don't know where you are." No one responds in a resonating way. The blank stares and the awkward laughs are nonverbal testimonies to this kind of isolation and loneliness.

Some loneliness is the unavailability of people to communicate with on any level. But loneliness is also experienced when there is no one to communicate with at your level of awareness (whatever that level may be). I'm sure that this kind of loneliness plagued Paul. There were few who really understood him. No matter how much he extended himself, he found few people who "knew where he was." He walked a lonely road, always looking for pilgrim companions. This loneliness is shared by all who individualize faith. As faith becomes more personalized and distinct, our relationship with God becomes closer even as the need for understanding companions becomes more acute.

Somehow, Paul made the most of his loneliness. Out of his feelings of abandonment and isolation came a new appreciation for his relationships with the Thessalonians and the tenacity to stick with them. He experienced the separation to its fullest. Allowing himself to accept his aloneness opened up his willingness to risk deeper relationships.

The emotional atmosphere of these verses is intense. The feelings of separation and abandonment had become unbearable. "Bear it no longer" (3:1) carries the hint of no longer covering up feelings. Paul was saying, "When I could hide my feelings no longer," or, "I can't stand it anymore. I must know how you are doing." It is as difficult for us as it was for Paul to show our need for attention from others. Athens may have been the test of

Paul's ability to sustain relationships. Paul was saying that he could no longer shelter or conceal his feelings. The word for "bear it" denotes a deliberate silence, an ability to keep a secret, to hide or to conceal, or to protect or hold in by covering up. What a graphic expression of how we hide our feelings! By covering up, we are able to keep away something that threatens. Paul was saying that he could no longer do that.

Being left behind carries the same stark theme of abandonment found in 2:17. The same word is used of leaving loved ones at death (see Mark 12:19). Linked with "at Athens alone," the depth of Paul's feelings of separation are shown. Paul's dependency on others for sympathy and support is clearly evident. On the surface, Athens should have been a stimulating place. It was the intellectual capital of the world. Paul could have matched his mind with some of the great minds of his time. But that only intensified his loneliness, for there was a great gulf fixed between the intellectualism of others and Paul's emotional and affectional needs.

My only experience in keeping a journal was during a period of loneliness. It was precipitated by illness and a delayed diagnosis of mononucleosis. The accumulated effect of illness and stress had taken its toll. It was bad enough being forty-three years old! The doctor said that I could continue my activities at a slower pace so I decided to keep a commitment to teach a month at Midwestern Baptist Theological Seminary. The journal begins with leaving home on Sunday afternoon and ends with returning home late the following Friday evening.

The journal is quite ordinary. It follows no rules of journal keeping and holds no extraordinary insights. But it reflects a search for community and support during an anxious period when resilience was at a low ebb. Paul's experience of being "alone in Athens" was constantly on my mind. The following portions are from my reflections on loneliness, taken word for word from the journal.

Sunday, 1:30 PM. I left home crying, not knowing why. I had left a hundred times before. Melissa said, "We never acted like this when Daddy left before." It was an emotional experience. I didn't want to leave, feeling alone and afraid. Driving through the city, I was tempted to turn around and go back. When I passed the last Nashville exit, I felt as if a part of my life was behind me and that I was leaving it for good.

Monday, 1:00 PM. I arrived at the seminary and picked up the key to my room. I was dead tired, aching, and exhausted from the drive. I tried to rest, but my heart started beating rapidly and the cold sweats came again. I began to say over and over in my mind, *I can't do it, I can't do it. I need to be at home. I'm sick. There's something wrong with me!* I made a decision to call Lela and tell her to come and get me. I called and the line was busy. I called again and the line was busy. I began to cry. I called again and again, and the line was busy. I put down the phone, and it rang. It was Jim, calling to discuss my Equipping Center conferences. I finally got myself together. It was good that he called because it brought me back to reality and helped me pull myself together. I thought about my single friends in the Sunday School class. It was remarkable to me how well they seemed to cope with loneliness and how poorly I seemed to be handling it.

I felt that I couldn't stay in the room. I needed to be around people at night that cared for me. I needed supports. When I was alone, I was afraid and anxious. I tried to call Bonnie and Ernie but no answer. Finally, I reached Harold and Eva Marie. I told them about my need. I planned to spend the night with them on Tuesday.

5:00 PM. I went to the cafeteria to eat, feeling very isolated. I saw Ernie in a classroom, and my spirits lifted. We talked at supper, went to the room, and called Bonnie. I began to feel better. But after Ernie left, the weariness began to hit me again. I tried to lie down, feeling feverish and extremely depressed. I began to panic. Ernie mentioned as he left that Ben was at Baptist Hospital. I felt that I couldn't make it through the night without some help. I called Baptist Hospital and said that I had mononucleosis and needed to be examined. I really thought I would be in the hospital for a week at least. I made plans to cancel the class and wondered how I would get home. I was sure that they would diagnose something serious. I guess I didn't plan to return to the room because I locked the key in it! I spent two hours at the hospital and was thoroughly checked. Nothing serious warranted my stay in the hospital. But the doctor did prescribe medication. I got back to the seminary at eleven o'clock, managed to find a key to the room, and went immediately to bed. I slept until two-thirty, got up and read until four o'clock, and went back to bed and slept lightly until seven.

Tuesday, 7:00 AM. Class begins today. I feel surprisingly good with little sleep. I have decided to begin the journal and share it with the class during the month. I read some of the Psalms. "O Lord, heal me, for my bones are troubled" (Ps. 6:2). "I am weary with my moaning;/every night I flood my bed with tears;/I drench my couch with my weeping. My eye wastes away" (Ps. 6:6).

12:00 Noon. There are twelve in the class—the right number. Although I was psyched up emotionally, my body was already tired. I didn't feel that I had the dynamic that I usually have when I teach. It's a good group. We contracted about classwork and shared expectations. I decided that I could not lead in a dynamic way from a position of strength. I can lead with some dynamic from a position of weakness. I probably need the class more than they need me. I decided to share the diary periodically. After class I went back to the room and tried to rest some. The switchboard called and said that I had a package that needed to be picked up. I went to the switchboard, and there was a large basket of fruit from the Singles Sunday School class. One of the women in the office said, "Now who would care enough about you to do that?" A few tears came, then a laugh. I gave her an apple!

Wednesday, 6:30 AM. I have spent the night with Harold and Eva Marie. Harold prayed for normalcy for me at breakfast. I guess that's what I want. My own prayers are very simple, more heart cries. But I'm willing to learn from this experience. I pray that God will simply walk with me during the day and help me do a little less "walking" at night.

I'm feeling a little guilty about the class. I'm not fully into it with the intensity I would like to have. My mind is dull. I'm not responding well to questions. My lectures lack vibrancy. I must trust the group to do more for one another.

Friday, 12:00 Noon. Class went well today. We talked about spiritual gifts and did an exercise. During class it started to snow and by the time class was over, we were into a good old-fashioned, Kansas City blizzard. I hopped in the car and headed for the airport. The airport was in chaos and closed down. No flights came in or out for about four hours. I began to panic again. I thought that I would miss the last flight out of Saint Louis to Nashville and would have to stay in a Saint Louis hotel for the night or sit in the airport. I decided that I would sit in the airport rather than go to a lonely motel room. I hopped on the first flight I could get to Saint Louis, hoping I would make the connecting flight. In spite of the mononucleosis I began running through airports! The Saint Louis to Nashville flight was running an hour and a half late. We arrived at 10:45. I was home by 11:30. Lela and I talked to 1:00. I slept until 6:00—off and on till 8:00. Thus ended six interesting days in the middle of March 1979.

Community as Support (3:2)

Paul sent Timothy to the Thessalonians to build the bridge of community and to strengthen and establish their faith. Paul was willing to deprive himself of the constant fellowship with Timothy so that he might receive some message from the Thessalonians.

Timothy was not only a brother but also he was a fellow worker, a partner in the faith. Paul wanted the Thessalonians to know Timothy as a brother and fellow minister. In this situation he was an equal. Timothy's task was a faith-shaping mission. The Thessalonian's trouble should not cause them to lose heart or lack faith. Faith was the key issue. He was to establish and comfort them concerning their faith.

Community as "Buffer" to Personal Depression (3:3-5)

Faith is related to trouble. Christians are not to be strangers to trouble. Trouble is a great teacher of faith. There is much to learn that we can only learn the hard way. We do not often go to people who have the appearance of being on top of their troubles. There are qualities of character that are brought about only by trouble. Trouble is part of the process of learning the Christian life. It is so inevitable that Paul said "this is to be our lot." We are appointed to it (3:3). This is the same word that Jesus used to describe a city set on a hill in Matthew 5:14. We are set for trouble—for all the world to see.

The warnings about pressure have been stated clearly in 2:5. Paul had repeatedly stated that affliction is part of the Christian life. The Greek word for *affliction* is descriptive of pressure, a choking pressing feeling that represented the kind of trouble that crushes and squeezes out life and vitality. Actually, Paul was depressed. He was well acquainted with the physical discomfort that constantly plagued him. But here we are in touch with the emotional and spiritual aspects of his pain. We see Paul's own pain reaching out—his own need of belonging and acceptance. Someone has said that this kind of suffering (depression) is "world pain." It exists with all people in the midst of living.

The pain intensified his relationship to the Thessalonians with a special poignancy. He identified with their affliction by personally participating in it. Nothing binds people together like suffering. We do not have community because we have not learned to share pain. Emotional pain particularly brings every other feeling to a heightened level of awareness. Paul not only knew their pain but also shared their pain.

Here is the need of a helper to be helped. Suffering and helping are interchanging roles. We are now sufferers, now healers; now helpers, now being helped; now givers, now receivers. The experience of a community is always a reciprocal experience. Community is built on the basis of mutual need and care.

The intensity of his feeling is obvious. In verse 5, Paul repeated what he said in verses 1 and 2. "Because I can no longer stand the separation, I am sending Timothy to you."

Paul wanted some assurance that the Thessalonians were not weakened by their afflictions. Because of our vulnerabilities, others may seek to deceive us. We should not be flattered or cajoled with smooth talk in the midst of our difficulties. Trouble might lure us into betraying the faith. Others might wheedle it away from us through coaxing. We should not be "smooth talked into thinking that things will get better." Paul was challenging the Thessalonians to confront their troubles directly.

Satan, the tempter (3:5), is the master of tricky communication. He breaks up the road that would lead us to other people (2:18). He is the master manipulator with a full bag of deceptive surprises. Satan's mission is clear. He messes up the interpersonal! He knows the power of emotions in our lives so that is where he works!

"Ah! he has not been at work upon the human heart for nothing during these many thousand of years; he knows how to lull us to sleep to the best advantage, that he may take our thoughts and affections, and, above all, our passions, well into his keeping."[1]

Community as Good News (3:6-8)

"But now" in 3:6 begins a new thought. Timothy had brought back good tidings, had come "to us from you." The bond between the Thessalonians and the missionaries was strong. The expression "good news" in this context is remarkable. Nowhere else in the New Testament are these words used in any other sense than that of preaching the gospel. Paul heard the news as if it were "evangelism," the good news of the gospel. He moved from the despair of bereavement and abandonment to the joyful good news of their faith. His heart was full, and his anxiety was relieved.

"Good News of Your Faith and Love" (3:6). What was the good news? First, there was the news about the Thessalonians' faith. They had not wavered in maintaining growth in their faith. Paul's concern about their faith was a personal concern and a concern for his total mission. Their faith brought him life. Second, they continued in their love. Just as faith is Christians' attitude toward God, so is love Christians' attitude toward others. But love was not just a characteristic of the Thessalonians' lives. They loved Paul! Paul discovered that the people he loved also loved him. That was good news! Paul had feared that his converts might not love him in the same way that he loved them. But he was delighted to find that they "long to see us, as we long to see [them]."

The Thessalonians had not allowed any kind of tricky communication to distort their feelings toward Paul. They still looked back on his visit with them with great joy. But they did more than that. They looked forward with eager longing to a reunion and were just as anxious to see Paul again as he was to see them. The yearning to see another was mutual.

"We Have Been Comforted" (3:7). Faith was the catalyst that had produced the Thessalonians' love, loyalty, and commitment to Paul. "Your faith" is mentioned twice in 3:6-7. Their faith in God had brought new life to Paul. Their belief in God and their feelings toward Paul had given him courage. "Comforted" does not mean that he had been soothed but that he had been given new strength. The good news had literally washed over him

and had revitalized his energies to rise above his difficulties. Faith is contagious. Faith gives strength to others. Paul emphasized that fact again and again.

"We Live, if You Stand Fast" (3:8). Because of the Thessalonians' faith, Paul could stand fast in the Lord. He could feel alive again. Through his affliction and partly through the perils in which he often lived, the apostle said, "I die daily" (1 Cor. 15:31, KJV). But under the influence of the glad tidings from Thessalonica, he came to life. The implication is that if the faith of the Thessalonians had failed, if the church had broken up, it would have been a death blow to Paul and his mission. Paul said, "For now we live, if you stand fast in the Lord." The emphasis is on you—they were truly a test case. In Philippians Paul wrote, "For to me to live is Christ" (Phil. 1:21). But here he wrote, for me to live is you. At that time in his life, Paul needed to be reassured that the Thessalonians were being faithful to the gospel. Knowing that the Thessalonians were standing firm encouraged Paul in his mission.

Unfinished Business (3:9-13)

Before this section of 1 Thessalonians, Paul had expressed his feelings of abandonment. His loss came from uncertainty about the fulfillment of his hopes and expectations. When we become depressed, all the unfinished business comes into sharp focus. Whatever we have left behind is revived and lived again. When there is too much excess baggage of unfinished business, every movement becomes a matter of increasing complication.

But Paul experienced an emotional reversal. From the depths of depression, he rose to the heights of joy. He felt that this "rush of grace" came through the love of the Thessalonians. He used some form of the personal pronoun you no less than fourteen times in 3:6-13. There is no doubt who was responsible for this surge of new life.

Thankful to God for You (3:9)

Paul's first response was gratitude to God, for grace alone had made this possible. Paul was ready to return to God something for the joy he received. The Thessalonians loved him as much as he loved them. His joy went beyond all bounds.

Finish Your Faith (3:10)

When Paul saw the Thessalonians again, he did not simply want to revel in good fellowship. He purposed strengthening their incomplete faith. He wanted to be present among them in order to "supply what is lacking in your faith."

The word for "supplying" or "finishing" is translated in other places "equipping" (see Eph. 4:12). From this word, we get the word *artisan*, one who rounds out, completes, makes whole, or supplies what is lacking. Like any good artisan, Paul wanted to finish the task of maturing the Thessalonians in faith. He had been delighted in their response, but that did not mean that he was blind to their deficiencies or "lacking[s]." His love for them did not lessen his willingness to confront them.

What is this equipping task? What is needed to unite, round out, complete, and make whole? As far as Paul was concerned, there are two unfinished deficiencies—faithing and loving. All other equipping tasks are secondary. Our equipping methods often work the opposite way. We seek to equip people with every known skill and forget the primary task of faithing and loving. Our energies are depleted teaching/learning more methods and more tools at a time when people need more heart. The finishing touch is not a smooth gloss that hides a person's unique qualities. Faithing and loving have to do with substance, and we would often substitute that for style. Or, at least, we try.

"Direct Our Way to You" (3:11)

Paul's goal seems to have been to visit Thessalonica for an extended period of time with these people who had become so much a part of his life. He prayed that God would so guide the course of his work that he would be able to be with them again. "Direct our way" means to make a straight way or level way. Satan, the hinderer, had attempted to cut off the way. Paul gave the relationship back to God to remove the obstacles and to open up the way. But he probably began to realize that any time with them would be brief and that the "finishing" work would not be his to do.

Your Love Increasing and Abounding (3:12)

Paul recognized that the Thessalonians' growth in faith and love was in the Lord's hands. So he prayed that they might increase and abound in love, just as the grace of God had increased and abounded in him. There is no argument here between faith and love. Good loving is the fruitful evidence of good faithing. The words *increase* and *abound* are synonyms that express one idea—the overflow of love.

The grace of God spills over unto the magnificent abundance of love in our hearts. God does not dole out his love in sample packages. He floods us with it. The Thessalonians had experienced that love in such a way that it overflowed not only "toward one another" but "toward all."

The religious establishment has never known what to do with unchecked devotion and affection even in its most noble causes. Situations become too impulsive and too unpredictable, too warm, too heartfelt. Things are much more comfortable at a level of moderation and mediocrity. The model person is always prudent and self-possessed.

And so we live cautiously with affection, even when people around us dry up and die from the lack of it. We give people "love in general" which, in reality, is no love at all. Chrysostom, a fourth-century preacher, in commentary on this Scripture, said, "Do you see the unchecked madness of love which is indicated by these words." Growth in faithing and loving makes our interpersonal relationships exciting and unpredictable. Abounding has the meaning of an ocean of love that reaches the top edge of its borders and overflows.

Without love, the Christian community lives in drought. The river of life dries up, leaving huge beds of dry land with only small trickles to keep the stream alive. But when love abounds, the tributaries fill up and gradually the dry land in the river bed disappears. Finally, the flow of life-giving energies not only fills the channels but also overflows the banks and touches everything around it. When that happens, people become bold again. They sing new songs and speak new messages because the love that fills and overflows can no longer be contained. The faithing and the loving begin to do their work, the situation gets out of hand, and suddenly we have Acts 2 all over again.

"Establish Your Hearts" (3:13)

The purpose for abounding is given in this verse. Growth in faith and love will establish and buttress our hearts. "Hearts" does not simply refer to the emotions, but it is comprehensive of the whole inner life, including thinking, feeling, and willing. The whole personality is established, strengthened, and buttressed only when there is an overflowing abundance of faith and love.

Chapter 3 closes with Paul's acknowledgment that the people were made whole by faith and love in the presence of the Lord Christ. Notice Paul's reference to the presence of Christ among his people. When he appears, all the redeemed shall appear with him. His coming and the gathering of his people are one. And so we will all be together, along with the Thessalonians, in the Lord's good company.

4
The Body and Interpersonal Communication
4:1-18

Chapter 4 begins a discussion of the Christian's relationship to the body. The Christian faith often has been a disembodied faith. We need to be reminded that we are one person. Body and mind are one. My body is me, and my mind is me. Belief comes not from what is conceived in the brain but what is believed in the whole body. The Bible points to the unity of the person. It refuses to split the person into mind over body or head over heart. The Christian is not imprisoned with a division of flesh from spirit. I am free to be a person—one person.

Without this awareness of bodiness, a person is divided between body and spirit. The complete loss of body contact characterizes the schizophrenic state. The healthy person senses unity. My body is an expression of my total self—alive, vibrant, charged with feeling. People are often not aware of the lack of aliveness in their bodies. In fact, they think of the body as an instrument or a tool of the mind, and this relative deadness of body is accepted as a normal state.

Through my body, I belong to this world. It is also through my body that I will belong to the world to come. Through his discussion of resurrection, Paul's belief about the importance of the body becomes clear. Flesh and blood, as we know it, cannot inherit the kingdom. But the resurrected state will not be bodiless. There will be new bodies which we can only dimly comprehend now.

Spiritual health comes from "grace-full" body. We are most fully alive when the body is most alive and unburdened. Depression and psychosis are frequently connected with the lack of body integration. Wooden and mechanical behavior is born of a need to control the body. The grace of

God is mediated through bodiness. Here I am, all of me. Lumpy where I should be slim, dimpled where I should be round, wrinkled where I should be smooth. Here I am, "warts and all." My life is carried on through my body.

The Challenge to Please God (4:1-2)

Paul began this passage with three styles of interpersonal communication. He combined the words *beseech, exhort,* and *charge* (*instructions,* v. 2). He challenged the Thessalonians to live sanctified lives in respect to all people at all times. These strong verbs introduce the section of Paul's teachings about the body.

Paul underlined his teachings with a double injunction "we beseech and exhort you." The words imply a personal urgency and challenge. He wanted a response. "Beseech" means asking in the sense of requesting. "Exhort" has a sense of urging or encouraging. By using both words, Paul was asking, How shall all that we do in our daily lives be pleasing to God? Since the affectionate word "brethren" was used, the exhortation was friendly and assumed a positive response.

"In the Lord Jesus" is basic to the whole exhortation. Paul's authority came from the authoritative Christ. He was speaking what God willed for the Thessalonians. There is the power of God's authority behind his speaking. The Greek word for "instructions" (v. 2) is much like the one translated "charge" in 1 Timothy 1:5. A military command is given by an officer to stimulate the response of those in the ranks.

Paul was balancing sanctification, passion, and intimacy. He related sanctification to sexuality. He knew there was no wholeness in life without coming to terms with one's sexuality. We never get our lives straight until we get our bodies straight. We cannot divide the two. Paul was saying that our sanctification is tied to the sanctification of the body.

Paul had seen some growth in the Thessalonians. He thanked God for what had already been obtained, but there was room for more. This abounding is in all directions. It implies the freedom and spontaneity of growing up in all ways.

Sexuality and Our Whole Lives (4:3-10)

This Is the Will of God, Your Sanctification (4:3)

Sanctification is the process of holiness. It is simply becoming whole. From the moment we believe, we become set apart for God. We have given our lives over to God to do his will. The old ways and the old habits are put behind us and replaced with the new ways. We center our lives more and more around the purposes of God. This is a long process, but it is necessary for the life "on this side" and prepares us for life on "the other side." Paul tied sanctification to the whole of the Christian life. That is why he used terms like "walk" and "abound." Paul commonly used these words to refer to the whole of a person's manner of living. They refer to a continual, if unspectacular, pilgrimage which characterizes the Christian way.

Something happens to us in sanctification, but there are no formulas and really no examples of what it will be like. There are no adequate categories to describe the process and dynamics of sanctification. People will always find remarkably new ways to be Christian. There are no patented patterns of human activity (no twelve steps) that can produce sanctification. Spiritual growth always points to the sovereignty of the Spirit's work. Our hope is that God "who began a good work in [us] will bring it to completion" (Phil. 1:6). Progress, but not the awareness of progress, is necessary in our growth. Awareness of growth can become the greatest obstacle to growth, just as we lose humility when we seek to claim it.

Growth in holiness is paradoxical. It may be that the more we work at it, the more we lose it. Those who covet the image of godliness often concentrate on a personal trait that is the opposite of a personal weakness. Mastering the sex drive may be equal to overcoming sin. If anger is the Achilles' heel, a calm disposition may be the pinnacle of Christian growth.

When we identify sanctification with certain personal traits or "indicators," we distort the meaning of sin and redemption. When the personal trait is achieved, we may be nearer to the kingdom of God, or we may not be. If I conquer the whole world, will I have arrived? Wholeness and completeness will not be found in this life because Paul said it is related to our bodies.

The Body as Vessel (4:4)

The Greek word translated "wife" is *skeuos,* meaning "vessel." Some commentaries believe that this reference is to the body as a "vessel," meaning "take care of your own body in holiness and honor." I do not want to get into that argument. Rather, I would like to work with the image of vessel as a good picture of how we relate to our bodies.

I can identify with Paul's image of the body as vessel. The more popular term for body in most New Testament studies is *temple.* I have seen a few bodies that I thought were "fearfully and wonderfully made" (KJV), and even fewer remind me of temples. A vessel is more realistic: temporary, cracked, fragile, and often disfigured. That's the kind of body that I know.

"We have this treasure in earthen vessels," said Paul in 2 Corinthians 4:7. The word for *vessel* found in 1 Thessalonians 4:4 and 2 Corinthians 4:7 may be translated "pot." In 2 Corinthians 4:7, we are pots of earthenware that contain the treasure of God. This treasure is the light of God. Our bodies are the light's containers, fragile vessels of earth. Paul possibly was referring to the clay lamps that were commonly used to hold the light. He might even be referring to the pottery used in the sacrificial system. Whatever, these earthen vessels contain the treasure of God and therefore should be moving toward holiness and sanctification.

I remember clearly the sermon that propelled me toward Christian vocation. It was under the hot, steamy pavilion roof at Baptist Hill outside of Mount Vernon, Missouri, in July 1956. I sat night after night in that old tabernacle under the preaching of Clyde Francisco. Most of these sermons were exegetical messages, coming directly from an Old Testament text. I was deeply touched one night by his sermon on Jeremiah 18:1-6. Jeremiah went to the potter's house and saw the potter working on a vessel, molding this vessel for his own purposes. The clay is pliable and flexible in the potter's hand. Suddenly the vessel becomes marred and disfigured, and the potter had to rework it as "seemed good" to do. Then came the word of the Lord, "Behold, like the clay in the potter's hand, so are you in my hand, O house of Israel." When the invitation came that night, I was ready to go anywhere and do anything.

Paul spoke from his own experience when he said that the power of God triumphed through weakness. Although Paul may have wanted to be a temple, like most of us, he was more like a vessel of earth. A second-century letter gives this picture of Paul: "'A man of moderate stature, with curly [or crisp] hair and scanty; crooked legs; with blue eyes; and large knit eyebrows; long nose; and he was full of the grace and pity of the Lord, sometimes having the appearance of a man, but sometimes looking like an angel.'"[1]

I have never had the illusion that my body looked like a temple. The fact is, it is misshaped—short arms and legs, thick waist, and a short neck set on broad shoulders. "Squatty body" was a tag put on me when I played church softball, and that name still follows me around at times. The body as a vessel of earth often reminds us that it is not a permanent structure. Life is uncertain and brief. Muscular development decays quickly. This body tells us that the body of the future life will be a changed body, no longer subject to the ravages of time and disease.

The body as a vessel is a more fitting interpretation of this verse than a man taking a wife as a vessel. The fact is, both are vessels carrying the light of God. For our sanctification every man must have only his own wife and every woman only her own husband (1 Cor. 7:2). In fact, Paul's boldest statement about marital intimacy is that the husband's body belongs to the wife and that the wife's body belongs to the husband (1 Cor. 7:4).

Whatever authority we have over our own bodies has been transferred equally to the other. Our bodies are "in debt" to each other. This concept of vessel does not degrade either one. Vessel simply reminds us of our earthliness, how funny our bodies really look, and how they are neither to be worshiped nor devalued. The body as vessel is both very serious and very funny. I can remember times that Lela and I have roared in laughter about our bodies. And why not? They are funny! So, we can say that the use of the word vessel implies both the male and female bodies. Both find sanctification in bodily life through seeking to do God's will.

"The Passion of Lust" (4:5)

We are not to deal with our sexuality as the pagan's do, "not in the passion of lust like the heathen who do not know God." Passion for Paul was an ungovernable desire like a fire that rages out of control. "In passion of lust" means to be carried away by passion. Lust is like a fire that one encourages and feeds.

Although passion is used by Paul in a negative sense, we must not negate its importance. Passion is necessary to the vital Christian life. Without passion there is apathy. Apathy results in coolness and a total lack of feeling of any kind. Apathy results from feelings that are restrained or separated from bodily life. There is no warmth toward others. There is no anger toward others. If feelings have any location at all, they are located in the head.

Emotions are passions in that they are feelings that flow as powerful movements of energy through the body and into the world. Emotions and passions involve intense bodily awareness. Passion allows our feelings to come out into the open. Perhaps the most profound example of passion was Jesus' cry on the cross, "My God, my God, why hast thou forsaken me" (Mark 15:34b). At that moment, he was overwhelmed by intolerable feelings of abandonment and despair.

Instead of ignoring my feelings of passion, I acknowledge that they are my own. I feel them in my heart and in my gut and in my head and in my hands and in my feet. I am these passions. They belong to me. Passion is a refusal to repress such feelings. It is a refusal to submit to apathy. Apathy is similar to what the ancient Stoics felt in that the only feelings that were permitted are those which are kept under the strict control of reason.

Passions must be channeled and shaped so that they energize and vitalize a whole range of activity. Without passion, there is no energy. Passion comes from a generous heart which feels at times that it would be filled to overflowing with a warmth of feeling.

This is different from lust. Lust is an overmastering feeling of want and desire. It has the same intensity as passion but it is directed toward a single object. The intensity of it overwhelms and masters us. We have no control over it. It is just as Jesus said. When we look at another with lust, it is as if we had already done the act because lust will lead us to the consummation of the act. Lust includes every excessive and unlawful desire that leads us away from sanctification and wholeness. The lust for money carries with it the same uncontrollable desire as the lust for flesh. It delays the process of holiness. It sidetracks the journey of the pilgrim. We must leave it behind.

The Results of Sexual Looseness (4:6-8)

Paul pictured the results of uncontrolled feelings in three ways. When we lose all control of our feelings, we defraud our brothers and sisters, ourselves, and the Holy Spirit.

Against Your Brother (4:6). Lust leads us to go too far. We covet. We become greedy, we overreach, we defraud, we oppress. The Phillips translation says, "You cannot break this rule without cheating and exploiting your fellow-men." The word translated "transgress" means "to overreach." We take something that does not belong to us. We overreach the bounds of our lives and spill over in hurtful ways into the lives of other people.

Against Your Whole Life (4:7). The word "uncleanness" describes the opposite of sanctification. The one is as broad as the other. Uncleanness refers not only to sexual sin but to other sin as well. Just as sanctification includes far more than sexual purity, uncleanness describes the whole form of pagan life. Sanctification describes all that is new in the Christian life. But the importance of sanctification to sexuality is a key. Carl Jung once remarked that when people brought sexual questions to him, they invariably turned out to be religious questions. And when they brought religious questions to him they turned out to be sexual ones. Sexual questions have an inevitable religious dimension. We cannot divide sexuality from sanctification and wholeness. Both sanctification and sexuality have to do with our "whole lives."

Against the Holy Spirit (4:8). We not only sin against a code of ethics given to us by God but also we sin against God, in the present moment, who has given us the Holy Spirit. When we "disregard" God, we hold all that he is as null and void. Paul said, "The body is not meant for immorality, but for the Lord, and the Lord for the body" (1 Cor. 6:13). The freedom and spontaneity of bodily life come through the purposes of God who is for us. As we respond to his love, we are set free to be loving persons. When we declare null and void his purposes, we become slaves of our own passions and lusts. The purpose of our sexuality is that we may know intimate love that is expressed through our whole being. Any other use of our sexuality will not free us but enslave us. We are free to be complete people through our bodies within God's purposes.

The Fine Line Between Emotional Intimacy and Sexual Laxity (4:9-10)

What are the principles that Paul was setting forth in 1 Thessalonians 4? First, we are reminded that our sanctification (wholeness) is closely related to our sexuality. There is no spiritual maturity that is not related to our bodies. Paul's first teachings were warnings. We are to "abstain from unchastity." We are to treat our "vessels" (our bodies and the bodies of our spouses) in holiness and honor. We are not to feed the fires of lust. Our sexual looseness offends others, ourselves, and the Holy Spirit. Simply stated, we are not called by God for uncleanness, but for holiness (4:7). We live in the context of relational limits.

Love One Another (4:9). At the same time, we are challenged and admonished to love the brethren. The "brethren" is to be interpreted as the church, the community of faith, all those called together by God, both men and women. The Thessalonians had been taught by God to love one another, and to a certain degree they learned to do that. But Paul challenged them "to do so more and more" (4:10).

Because love is valued so highly in the church, counterfeit love is often passed out as the real thing. The lack of love hides behind the mask of love and words that sound like love. That is why Paul said that love should be genuine (Rom. 12:9). Deep down we all know the secret about love; it cannot be faked. Therefore, it must be filled with real feeling and emotion. Expressions of love without feeling is hypocritical and false.

We love with and through our bodies. This is scary. It means letting our bodies express what our minds and hearts feel. But we often feel that our bodies will betray us. We are afraid that if our bodies take over, they will expose our weaknesses, demolish our pretentiousness, reveal our passions and lusts, and vent our fury. Like it or not, our bodies express our relationships to others—from the fleeting and casual to the lasting and intense; from the relatively impersonal to the deeply personal. Physical expression exists on a continuum, from varied types of eye contact and casual touch to different forms of embrace and sexual expression. In one way or another, we inevitably express our sexuality in every human relationship.

Abounding in It (4:10). The Thessalonians were a loving people. But Paul exhorted them to abound in it, "to do so more and more." We cannot follow Paul's admonishing without struggling with relationships between men and women in the church. Entering into such friendships seems risky. Friendships mean venturing out of my self-isolation into the depths of another person's life and exposing myself to influences which I may have difficulty controlling.

Friendship means a delicate balance between privacy and freedom. Love is an expression of affection. Affection is an embodied feeling, a passion. When I feel affection, I feel it in my body, and I want to express it through my body. I want to see and hear and touch and embrace. Sometimes affection involves feelings of sexual attraction. When it does, the other elements in friendship provide the boundaries of behavior so that feelings can be acknowledged without necessarily being acted upon. In many attempts at friendship, the desire to touch is not acknowledged, and the contact between people is purely "heady" or "intellectual." The repression of affection inhibits the growth of other elements in friendship.

Let me be clear. Our bodies become the best tools for achieving genuine communication with those around us. If you observe those who have deep relationships, you will find that although a few of them are indiscrimate "grabbers" who hug everyone in sight, most have a delicately tuned sense of touch, and it is in use every time they are with people. They listen with their eyes, draw close to other persons during conversation, and gesture frequently to keep the communication at a warm level. This is what Paul was talking about in 1 Thessalonians 2:7-8.

What do we do then when *eros* comes out of hiding and we find ourselves sexually drawn to others? If we are committed to closeness and to warm expressions of affection and if we are open to the feelings of others, sexual attraction may happen.

We cannot deny that emotional intimacy with someone of the opposite sex is potentially explosive. Opposite-sex friendships seem to be the most difficult to cultivate and to maintain. For some people, these friendships may develop into romantic or sexual relationships. For others, relationships may stagnate as the result of the fear of illegitimate intimacy. But these do not have to be the only ends to opposite-sex friendships. When real fellowship in church life creates close friendships, sexual feelings may begin to emerge. When we do not deal plainly with these feelings in ourselves and in others in an open way, much confusion can result. Avoidance is one way out of the dilemma, but it is costly. Relationships become emotionally shallow. Meaningful and potentially wholesome relationships are prevented from developing. At the most, avoidance keeps us from Paul's exhortation to abound in love for one another more and more.

The only way to overcome the confusion that results from sexual feelings within opposite-sex relationships is to remind ourselves of Paul's ultimate goal to build strong Christian communities. Community is the final word in Christian interpersonal relationships, not maleness and femaleness. These differences color and condition relationships in community. But the fact that men and women are Christians is more important than the fact that they are men and women.

We are a part of a new creation, a new humanity, members of Christ's body, sons and daughters of God, forming our lives together out of our love of Christ. As a part of this new family of faith, we are related to one another as brothers and sisters. Our relationship is characterized by love, affection, loyalty, and just plain "fun." Because of our family relationship, there is limited physical intimacy. But there is the potential for a depth of relationship that is not built on physical attraction. Certainly the relationship should be more than casual, polite, and proper. What kind of family is that?

This book is dedicated to Lela, my wife. She is the one. She is my glory and joy (1 Thess. 2:20). As far as genital love is concerned, she is the only one. But she is not the only woman in my life, nor do I honor her by saying so. For we both look for community, a body, a relationship of brothers and sisters. This community can best be called a family, where persons relate comfortably and freely, where others are cared for and served, and where God will make better lovers of us all.

The Body and Interpersonal Life (4:11-17)

The Body in Everyday Life (4:11-12)

In these verses, Paul set forth very practical considerations about the spiritual quality of our lives. The presentation of myself to others in everyday life is through my body. My whole body, or my total person, communicates. I am known through my actions. The impressions I leave with others are subtle, picked up through a multitude of verbal and nonverbal expressions.

Paul suggested that there is spiritual power in the common elements of everyday living. The deeper spiritual realities do not come only to those who spend large amounts of time in prayer and meditation. Who among us will ever be spiritual giants in study and contemplation? The deeper things of the Spirit also come in ordinariness, to those who have jobs, keep up homes, care for children, and absorb themselves in seemingly mundane tasks. There is hope for us. The spiritual realities happen in the midst of these ordinary daily activities.

In another way, Paul was drawing boundaries and placing limits on spectacular spiritual activity. He was calling for an inward simplicity which results in an outward bodily expression that is more direct and less "showy."

"*Aspire to Live Quietly*" (4:11) is a striking paradox. The word "aspire" or "study" (KJV) has a meaning of being ambitious. Therefore, Paul's remark is something like "be ambitious to be unambitious." This phrase might be translated "strive eagerly not to strive" or "seek restlessly to be still."

God has made us for simplicity and quietness. We devise duplicity, complexity, and frantic activity on our own. Our fragmentation comes because we burden ourselves with increased complexity. Simplicity and quietness is an inward reality that results in an outward life-style. We cannot hide it. It will show in a visible expression of behavior.

Paul was saying that living quietly takes effort. An inner control is a key to quietness. We are challenged to watch over both our verbal and nonverbal expressions. When basketball players lose their precision and rhythm, they are said to be playing "out of control." The energy and enthusiasm is there, but it has no focus. A tremendous amount of energy is needed to harmonize all aspects of our lives. That was Paul's point in "striving toward quietness." It is the "vital balance" that gives order to our living.

"Mind Your Own Affairs" (4:11). The best way to maintain peaceful lives is for persons to be intent upon their own duties and their own callings. When we turn aside from our own business and meddle too much in the things of others, disorder is the result. Paul was not saying to be unconcerned for others. He simply warned about dealing too much in idle curiosity about the lives of others. When idle curiosity gets the best of us, we become open disturbers of the peace.

Hidden in John 21 is one of Jesus' most difficult teachings on discipleship. Jesus challenged Peter to feed and tend the flock of God. For Peter, his own calling was to be enough. But I think it was not. Something else began to gnaw at him.

Seeing John following close behind them, Peter said to Jesus, "Lord, what about this man? (John 21:21). Here is the danger. Christians who are active, energetic, and committed tend to have exaggerated ideas of their responsibilities. They take on their shoulders the burdens of the whole world and appoint themselves to manage everything and everybody. Here again is a principle of limit and restriction—our responsibilities are best confined to narrow boundaries. None of us has unlimited responsibilities. We contribute best and most effectively to the whole by managing our own lives. Once we begin to look after and manage other people, it won't be long before we are trying to manage the Lord himself!

Jesus' response to Peter, "What is that to you? Follow me," is a firm reminder to all Christians. We are to live by the will of Jesus for our lives. That frees us from the urge to plan and control either our own lives or the lives of others. "Follow me" is both the first word of discipleship (Mark 1:17) and the last (John 21:22).

"Work with Your Hands" (4:11). Paul urged the Thessalonians toward the discipline of labor. Practically speaking, we should work to support our lives and the lives of those we love. Secondly, honest work builds community and provides an active witness before unbelievers. When Paul spoke about working with our hands, he was using the part for the whole. Certainly he included all worthy occupations of life. When all things are

done in service to Christ, honest work provides a visible expression of living quietly and minding our own business. Work is good for us. It is doubtful that those who cannot find spiritual strength through work will find it at other times. The Greeks looked down on manual labor as something that was beneath them. However, Christian faith did not hesitate to insist on the dignity of manual labor (Eph. 4:28).

"Command the Respect of Outsiders" (4:12) gives our lives a visible and simple quality. We live in an age of Christian celebrities where egos are overstimulated by excessive attention. There will always be super-Christians among us who live by exception. They do not have time for the common elements of daily living. But it is through these common elements that Christian character is built and provides us with the most immediate contacts with those on the outside. Our experiences say that this is true. The Christians who hold the most respect among unbelievers are those who live quietly, mind their own business, and work hard.

Have Need of Nothing (4:12). Attachment to things is insatiable. We buy things we do not need and soon weary of them. Paul warned against all addictions. Is there anything that we can't do without? Get rid of it immediately. Do we need to own things to enjoy them? It is a trap! For the last ten years I have run the streets of Nashville and the many state parks that are only two to three hours away from the city. In a sense, they are mine, but I neither possess nor control any of them. They all belong to me, and they are all free!

The Body in Resurrected Life (4:13-17)

The Separation from Interpersonal Life (4:13-15). Paul began this section with a statement that he did not want believers to be ignorant. He used this introduction before (Rom. 1:13; 1 Cor. 10:1; 2 Cor. 1:8). To be ignorant about spiritual reality leaves believers in a weakened condition. There is nothing to fortify and strengthen in time of need.

In this case, the Thessalonians were uncertain about the body in the life to come. They were anxious about loved ones who had died. They lived in a world without hope. According to Greek thought, there was no future for the body, which was regarded as a "prison house for the soul." Apart from Christian faith, there is no firm hope for life after death. The

Greeks talked about life after death, but they did not glory in it as did the Christians. In the second century AD, a certain Irene wrote a letter to a family in mourning. She cried over her friend's departed one, but she concluded her letter by saying: "Against such things, one can do nothing. Therefore, comfort yourselves."

How do we comfort one another without a belief in bodily resurrection? Christian comfort is no mystical speculation on life after death. It is based on the resurrection of the body. There is little comfort in a resurrection of souls and spirits. The New Testament does not teach the resurrection of the spirit; it teaches the resurrection of the dead. The resurrection of the dead is a resurrection of a spiritual body.

Paul spoke of the dead as being "asleep," the same term for death that was used by Jesus in Mark 5:39; Luke 8:52; and John 11:11. In the New Testament, there are two distinct teachings about death. On the one hand, death is most natural—like sleeping. On the other hand, it is completely unnatural—horrible, the last enemy, the result of sin. Christ in his death bore the wages of sin and endured the worst of all deaths. Christ is not described as sleeping. Christ died.

Therefore, Christ transformed the whole experience for those who are in him. Because he died, there is no horror in death for his people. Christ not only died but also rose again. The resurrection was a great event which demonstrated that death was not really all there is. The power of God is behind the resurrection. The same God who raised Jesus from the dead will also raise from the dead those who belong to Jesus.

To Paul, the departed ones were very real. They were persons. They are definitely alive and active. They are persons whom Jesus will bring with him from heaven at his coming. They are not spirits, but actual live resurrected bodies formed like the resurrected body of Jesus. There is no thought that these departed ones would be in glory while their bodies would remain buried. This is the attitude of the heathen who have no hope with respect to the body. Death brings their separation from us in that it is only through our physical bodies that we can relate interpersonally. But the reunion of interpersonal life is based on the power of God to change all of us into new bodies.

What do we know about the spiritual body? What are our clues about life in a resurrected body? We do have a clue—the Lord Jesus. He is the only one who has been resurrected in a spiritual body. If we are to understand the spiritual body, we will have to understand something about the resurrected body of Jesus. For our promise is that our bodies will be like his.

Now what was Jesus' body like? To answer that question we must look in Luke 24. He was the same person, but he was also different. Luke 24:31 says, "Their eyes were opened and they recognized him." His spiritual body was recognizable by those who followed him. Then it says that "he vanished out of their sight." Although he was recognizable and identifiable, he was not tied to the physical conditions like our bodies. He appeared and disappeared. He walked through closed doors. There were no barriers big enough, long enough, wide enough, or thick enough to keep him out of relationship with those he loved. Two of his followers said to each other, "Did not our hearts burn within us while he talked to us on the road" (Luke 24:32).

Jesus appeared again as the two from Emmaus were telling the followers in Jerusalem who they had seen. They were startled and frightened and supposed that they saw a spirit.

> He said to them, "Why are you troubled, and why do questionings rise in your hearts? See my hands and my feet that it is myself; handle me, and see; for a spirit has not flesh and bones as you see that I have." And while they still disbelieved for joy, and wondered, he said to them, "Have you anything to eat?" They gave him a piece of broiled fish, and he took it and ate before them (Luke 24:38-43).

Paul's initial experience with Christ on the Damascus road was in some sense an encounter with Christ in his spiritual body. His relationship to Christ was based on an experience with Christ's spiritual body. His relationship was very concrete and very powerful. Paul believed in resurrected bodies because of his relationship to Christ.

Paul wanted to make clear that one group of believers will have no advantage over another in the resurrection. All are united with Christ and with one another. The procession of those who rise is not the issue. (Someone has said that the reason the dead rise first is that they have six feet further to go!) I do not know the order or the direction of the procession. On that day, who will care? Here comes believers in Christ Jesus! Everything nailed down is coming loose. Everything loose is coming together. All believers are united with Christ and with one another. Interpersonal life will be restored. Those who are dead in Christ will be united with those who are alive in Christ, and the connection will be made through spiritual bodies.

The Reunion with Interpersonal Life (4:16-17). Alec Vidler says, "The true Christian feels himself to be living between the lightening of Christ's first coming and the thunder of his final appearing."[2] We celebrate his first coming and live in anticipation of his second coming. Living in anticipation keeps that vision alive in our minds and hearts.

The Lord's return will happen with a shout, a word of command. This same word describes the shout of a rider to his horses or the hunter to his hounds. It is the cry of the ship's master to the rowers and the commander to his soldiers. Always there is the ring of authority and the note of urgency. With a command, a shout, and a blast from the trumpet, Jesus will come down from heaven. The Lord's coming will be open, public, and not only visible but also audible. The descent of Christ seems to be characterized in the same way as his ascent to heaven. "This Jesus, who was taken up from you into heaven, will come in the same way as you saw him go into heaven" (Acts 1:11).

When Jesus comes, all things and all his people will begin to come together in him. Paul said that we will be caught up together in clouds. The words "caught up" (snatched, seized, carried off) express the idea of force, the irresistible power of God. We are not just caught up with him, we are caught up together with all those who have gone before. The coming of Christ will not only be a reunion with Christ but will also be a reunion with friends who have gone before. We are caught up together, bodily. The same word for "caught up" is used for Philip, the evangelist, who was caught away with the Spirit of the Lord in Acts 8:39. The same words describe a man in Christ who is caught up to the third heaven in 2 Corinthians 12:2-4.

In a twinkling of an eye, in the dramatic suddenness and swiftness of a series of events, we will all be changed. Paul said that the dead will be changed, but those of us who are alive will be changed also. In 1 Corinthians 15:51, Paul expanded on this idea. He called the transformation a mystery. "We shall not all sleep, but we shall all be changed." We shall all be transformed. The word *changed* means "made different or made another." We shall all be other than what we are now. Those sudden unpredictable transforming moments that we experience are preludes to that moment when everything becomes different. Those miraculous surges of the grace of God are wonderful previews of the grace that becomes all in all. How do we prepare for it? By keeping alive our capacity to be surprised by grace!

I am reminded of Oliver Wendell Holmes' description of a carriage, which is really an image of the human body. On the first of November 1855, the carriage was one hundred years old. That morning the parson got in the carriage and took off for a meeting. Now read about the death of the carriage.

> All at once the horse stood still,
> Close by the meet'n'-house on the hill.
> First a shiver, and then a thrill,
> Then something decidedly like a spill—
> And the parson was sitting upon a rock,
> At half past nine by the meet'n'-house clock,—
> . . . .
> What do you think the parson found,
> When he got up and stared around?
> The poor old chaise in a heap or mound,
> As if it had been to the mill and ground!

I really like that. The old carriage finally just gave it all up. The drying up, aging process just finally took its toll, and the carriage went back to dust.

> . . . it went to pieces all at once,—
> All at once, and nothing first,—
> Just as bubbles do when they burst.[3]

What a way to go!

The meeting in the air will be the reunion of spiritual bodies. The "to meet" was used in connection with an official welcome accorded newly arrived dignitaries. The welcome idea is strong here. The Lord will extend open arms, and the welcome will include all who belong to him. The raised as well as the changed shall ascend to meet the Lord in the air. The raised have different bodies, the changed have different bodies. All share together in the presence of the Lord, never to be separated from him or from one another. We are "with them . . . and with the Lord."

Comfort One Another (4:18)

Paul wrote all of this for a purpose. The purpose was (and is) to communicate comfort. We are to say these words to one another. We are to read these words of Scripture to one another. First Thessalonians says that we should constantly say these things to one another to provide comfort. With these words, we build a fortress of support around one another in times of despair and grief.

In our concern to provide a firm doctrine on the second coming, we often miss the main emphasis of this passage. The theme of the passage is the reunion of the believers with Christ and with those who have died. These images work at a powerful level in the minds of many Christians; and without images, it is impossible to communicate. Again, the theme of 1 Thessalonians is interpersonal communication. The apostle's aim is to calm and comfort the Thessalonians, not to propound a complete doctrine of last things.

I have a great fear of the decay of the physical body. My father had a stroke when he was seventy years old and was bedfast for eighteen years. I saw parts of his body twist, curl, and finally die in paralysis. When he died, there was not much body left. My mother had five cancer operations before she died. Two close friends bravely fought the cancer demon and lost. They were all living examples of the decay and destruction of the physical body.

By faith, I am ready to declare that they will be living examples of the glory and power of the spiritual body. This is my faith, alive in my imagination as it has been in the imagination of believers through the centuries. This body is perishable. But a day is coming when we believers shall all be changed. The body to come is like the body of the Lord Jesus. With this confession of faith and with these words, I would comfort you.

5
The Growth of Awareness
5:1-22

Awareness is the ability to see things that are unseen and to hear things that are unheard. Seeing and hearing were the first lessons that Jesus taught the disciples. They saw and heard the same things others did, but Jesus taught them to see and hear in a new way. New patterns of alertness must characterize the followers of Christ. It is not for us to know the times and the seasons that the Father has set within his own authority (1 Thess. 5:1; Acts 1:7). But through new ways of seeing and hearing, we will always be ready. Readiness comes through waiting, working, and watching.

The last chapter of 1 Thessalonians is reminiscent of many of the sayings of Jesus, particularly those found in Matthew 24. Although the Gospels had not been written, it is most likely that the sayings of Jesus, often spoken among his followers, were also being committed to writing by this time. The teaching of awareness was important to Jesus, and so it was with Paul.

The blinding light had struck Paul in such a way that he would never see things the same way again. As Christians, we are children of that Light. Matthew 24 tells us that the children of light will live in a new age. But the new age is visible only to those who can see it. Those who walk in darkness do not see the Light.

The new age will be consummated on that day of the Lord. Of the times and seasons, of that day and of that hour (1 Thess. 5:1; Matt. 24:36), we have no way of knowing. The Son will come like a thief in the night (1 Thess. 5:2; Matt. 24:43). Therefore, we must be on watch (1 Thess. 5:6; Matt. 24:42). Eating and drinking with the drunken (1 Thess. 5:7; Matt. 24:48,49) will dull our senses and will leave us ill-equipped for the suddenness of this event. Those with satiated senses are deaf and blind to eternity. But to those who can see and hear it, it is present already.

So let us sharpen our senses. Let us watch the fig tree (Matt. 24:32). By being observant, we can recognize the coming of spring before others are aware of it. In the same way, we shall discover the presence and work of Christ as soon as we learn to see him. Those who love the darkness will not see the signs. However, those children of Light, who keep on the watch, will learn to read the signs of the times. They will be prepared.

Jesus was not concerned with what was seen with the physical eye. He was wanting to develop faith eyes that would look into the secrets of the kingdom. "'To you it has been given to know the secrets of the kingdom of heaven, but to them it has not been given. . . . because seeing they do not see, and hearing they do not hear, nor do they understand'" (Matt. 13:11,13). For those who already see and hear, there is an inner hunger and thirst for spiritual things. When Jesus taught about the use of the senses (seeing and hearing, hungering and thirsting), he couched his words in parables. Parables are, on the surface, interesting stories. But beneath the stories are the basic descriptions of the inner life. The problem of the soil and the seed (Matt. 13) is not simply four groups of hearers but the understanding of our own inner situations. We discover the stones and thorns of the inner life that choke off the seed of the word from becoming fruitful. Awareness comes when the "seed-words" are seen and heard.

Awareness comes when we can be fully alive to the present situation rather than being concerned with what might be or what is absent. Awareness comes when we are able to accept what is unpleasant and painful, as well as what is pleasurable. Awareness comes when we do not try to restrict anything that God is trying to teach us.

Fully alive people are people who are alive in their external and internal senses. They see the world. They hear its music and poetry. They smell the fragrance of each new day. They taste the living bread of each moment. Their senses are offended by distortions and ugliness, but they do not blot out these experiences.

Fully alive people are also alive in their imaginations and emotions. They are able to experience the full gamut of human feelings—the wonder, love, awe, tenderness, compassion, the agony and ecstasy of life.

Fully alive people are alive in their minds. They are not afraid of new thoughts. They are able to learn from all their experiences without restricting either pleasure or pain.

Fully alive people are alive in their wills and hearts. They love God. They love themselves and, in deep and sensitive ways, they love others. This is the story of 1 Thessalonians 5. It is a remarkable manifesto of Christian freedom bringing into play a full awareness of the senses, the emotions, the mind, the will, and the heart.

Understanding Significant Events (5:1-3)

Quantity Time and Quality Time (5:1)

Awareness comes in our ability to distinguish between quantity time and quality time. Days and seasons are translations of two Greek words for time—*chronos* and *kairos*. Quantity time (*chronos*) is simply time in sequence. It is from this word that we get our word "chronology." It is calendar time and clock time, one thing following another. It can be measured through moments, days, periods, and hours. "How long have you lived?" is a question about *chronos* time. Most people eventually learn to tell *chronos* time.

Quality time (*kairos*) is different because it calls for interpretation. It is time that is tied to a specific event and locked in a definite time period. *Kairos* time is diffused with meaning, calling for reflection and meditation. "What happened to you?" is a question about *kairos* time. Many people never learn to tell *kairos* time.

Seeing things differently contrasts *chronos* time and *kairos* time. *Chronos* time is order and sequence. Do the first things first, take the next step, then the next. Don't waste time. *Kairos* time is promise and fulfillment. Start anywhere or take everything at once. For those who can see, everything has meaning. There is no such thing as wasted time.

The Day of the Lord (5:2)

Our growth in awareness is not the result of the mere passage of time. Our ability to keep in touch with what is going on hinges upon decisions made at decisive moments of opportunity. It is not *a* day. It is *the* day, like

D Day. This particular day, a point in time, has a special momentous place in my life.

Our perceptions of God's day shape our interpersonal lives and our personal goals. Growth is both gradual and cataclysmic. One day, one hour, one place, one person, and one event are all important. God breaks through the complexities and the distortions of our relationships and meets us in direct encounters. That is one way of describing God's day. All of these moments and days become preludes to the day of Jesus Christ.

The Lord's day may be a long way off or a sudden, immediate, intruding event in the midst of our own busy lives. Paul said, in effect, "You know accurately that you know nothing accurate as to the precise date for the day of the Lord." There is no way of knowing according to *chronos* time. The only way to understand God's day is through *kairos* time. To know precisely is the type of imagination with which Paul had no sympathy. Rather, he provided open images that are rich in symbolism but lacking in preciseness. We can only understand by perceiving through time which is significant and full.

Our awareness does not come all at once in a neat box. It comes piece by piece in messages marked through days. Each day brings a new piece to fit into the puzzle. Every new piece adds its own contribution to our deeper levels of awareness. We put these pieces together spasmodically. But the quality most needed for constructing this vision is an openness to what life brings and an avoidance of restriction. As long as our vision is open and flexible, we can keep accepting the new pieces of awareness that come to us.

False Security in Normality (5:3)

The day of the Lord comes like the labor pains of a pregnant woman. When the time is right, labor cannot be delayed. It calls for immediacy and urgency. The day of the Lord ushers in the birth of a new age, for in birth all things are becoming new. Awareness has a distrust of normality, knowing the powerful human longings for still waters and peace and safety. Beyond everything else, we often value the absence of alarm and conflict. But the very sharp and sudden birth pains demand immediate attention.

There is no way to ignore them. They are not only sudden but also are inevitable, and Paul warned us that they should not be unexpected in such a way that we are unprepared.

The desire for peace and safety are characteristics of people who lack awareness. Great energy is spent trying to keep everything on an even keel. The New Testament often characterizes peace as the well-being of the whole person. But here it means the absence of alarm or any potential conflict. *Safety* describes holding on to something that cannot be shaken or made unstable. Peace and safety are desires for protection from all outward obstacles. People of awareness know that turbulence is always just beneath the surface of things. Normalcy is mostly a delusion.

The great desire for peace and safety leads to boredom. *Boredom* is a noun derived from the verb *bore,* meaning to make a hole by boring. It results from grinding or digging a hole in something that was previously full and substantial. Boredom is the monotonous opening of a cavity until the space becomes empty, and that emptiness is called peace and safety.

Preparing for the Unexpected (5:4)

Paul returned to the image of Jesus' return that we see in Matthew 24:43 and Luke 12:39. The suddenness of his coming should not leave us unprepared.

If we see the kingdom only with the eyes of reason, it is marked by contradiction. It is near, yet it is not near. It is visible, yet it is invisible. It is marked by signs, yet it is known only to God. It is in the clouds of heaven, yet it is within the human heart. It grows slowly, yet it comes suddenly. We live in expectancy, yet it comes unexpectedly.

Awareness: Children of the Day (5:5-11)

Sons and Daughters of the Day (5:5)

People who walk in darkness miss so much. The children of Light will want to see it all. The sons and daughters of God belong to the light and the light belongs to them. The light is their natural home (Eph. 5:8,13,14). Because they carry the light, they must never forget the power of darkness. Light and darkness, day and night, are mentioned frequently by Paul and continue the theme of awareness.

The unaware live in darkness. They are surrounded by it and imbedded in it. Darkness is a part of their beings. Not only are they hidden from others but also they are hidden from themselves. Not so with those who belong to the light. The light has taken possession of God's sons and daughters. Their lives are characterized by light.

Watchfulness and Sobriety (5:6-8)

Because we walk in the day, our spiritual sensitivities are alive. Others may sleep, but those of the day are determined to be alert and awake. To be asleep is to die, to be awake is to live. So Paul urged wakefulness and sobriety. Sleep is characterized by spiritual and moral laxity and is an indication of not being prepared. The foolish virgins who had taken no oil for their lamps soon found the confusion of darkness (Matt. 25:3). Watchfulness is characterized by spiritual and moral alertness. The watchful person has the lamps burning brightly, looking forward to the return of the Bridegroom. We are to be aroused out of our tendency to sleep, lest through indolence we are unprepared (Matt. 24:42; 25:13) or error creeps into our thinking (Acts 20:29-31).

Soberness is characterized by spiritual and moral earnestness, which is neither overly excited nor indifferent. Soberness warns us that there are no emotional escapes. Soberness means the resistance to any type of intoxication. Intoxication causes an excess of self-indulgence and overexcitement. Sobriety is characterized by inner calmness and steadiness (1 Pet. 4:7). The sober person lives out of the depths of the soul, and the excitement comes from there rather than from the intoxication of outward stimulants.

Paul's concentration on watchfulness and calmness leads to the image of the sentry or guard. The sentry has all senses acutely tuned to the slightest sound. Because of the intensity of such concentration, there must be protection for the heart and mind. So Paul thought of the defensive armor of the breastplate (for the heart) and the helmet (for the mind). With this armor, the aware Christian puts on faith, love, and hope. This is the same order of these three, great workhorses as found in 1 Thessalonians

1:3. Faith, love, and hope increase awareness and protect against the seductions of the world.

A Personal Relationship with Christ (5:9-10)

Verses 9-10 bring the only mention in 1 Thessalonians of Christ's death for our salvation. He died for us so that we should live together with him. The verb "wake" in verse 10 is the word that is translated "watch" in verse 6. The word "sleep" in verse 10 is used of those who live unaware (v. 6-7). Moffatt translates these words "waking in life" and "sleeping in death." This verse provides further insight on the contrast between Paul's radical description of the children of light and the children of darkness.

Although Paul's doctrinal statement on salvation is short, it is complete. The relationship between Christ and his people is never terminated. This theme began in 4:14 and continues. Relationships developed with Christ and his people are not ended in death. Those who are in Christ will live "one and all" together with him. This is the same theme of togetherness found in 4:17. Those "caught up together" in him will "live with him."

Exhorting and Building Up (5:11)

Thoughts like those found in 5:11 will encourage and build up Christian fellowship. Paul said that these imperatives should be kept before the people continually and habitually. Encouragement comes from the power of these words in our lives. We must be reminded that exhortation and encouragement give people strength through the power of the spoken word. Through these words, we grow in spiritual stature and are built up. Notice again how "one another" receives special attention. We are to "encourage one another" and "build one another up." Together they emphasize the joyful, mutual responsibility that believers have for strengthening one another in faith.

Relationships Among the Strong and the Weak (5:12-14)

Awareness is bound up in my relationships with neighbor. The desire for "peace and safety" increases competition and hierarchical levels of interaction. Instead of loving our neighbors, we use them as ladders for self-elevation. Almost unconsciously, we begin to divide others into two camps—the strong and the weak. Paul probed this level of awareness.

Few relationships are equal in nature. There are some, but most have various degrees of strength and weakness. We relate to others at subtle levels of dominance and submission. This is a childhood pattern that is difficult to overcome. We see some people as parents, others as children. Transactional analysis did us a big favor by easily identifying these communication styles. There are few times when people gather that these relating positions don't come into play sooner or later.

One of the most profound experiences of my life was learning to relate as a peer to people who I perceived as having great strength. Growing up in church and seminary life provides us with constant interaction between people at all different levels and positions. Seminaries, colleges, and even churches have traditionally played into the hands of placing high value on position and titles. Teachers have profound positional authority in the lives of students. But a heavy dose of over-under relationships creates difficulty in learning for people.

I received a great gift when people I admired very much sought me out as a peer. In my younger student days, I stood in great awe of them, of their thoughts, of their writings, and of their leadership styles. Yet when they were willing to share some of their own inner lives and struggles with me, they became human beings. All the fathers began to topple from their pedestals. When they did topple, I perceived all people at a new level. There was no such thing as strong people and weak people—just people. Today I can honestly say I stand in awe of no man and only a few women!

In these short verses, Paul identified the wonderful Christian freedom in relating to people. The patterns of society are not the patterns that Christians are to follow, although we easily fall into them. Here are new ways of relating to the strong and the weak.

The Strong (5:12-13)

Informality is the key to Christian relationships as viewed from 1 Thessalonians. This is especially true of relationships with those who are perceived as leaders in churches. Formal structures in the church are usually based on informal contracts and agreements between people.

Know Them (5:12). First, Paul urged that we "know them" (KJV). This carries the idea of knowing fully, close up. Some people are difficult to know. But we are challenged by Paul to work at fully appreciating each leader in the church in informal, close-up ways. He characterized these leaders in three ways: "those who labor among you and are over you in the Lord and admonish you." These are not three different groups of people but all people who function as leaders.

The laborers "among you" are those who work hard in our midst. The preposition used here has significance. Work (toilsome labor) is done among, in the midst of, as a part of, side by side. This toilsome labor is the mutual ministry of the people of God—proclaiming the gospel, applying it to difficult situations, helping people in trouble, providing atmospheres for Christian growth. This kind of ministry requires strenuous effort, resulting in great weariness. The same Greek word for work or labor is used in 1 Thessalonians 1:3 and 2:9. It describes the great intimacy that develops among people who learn to work together. Again, Paul balanced the heavyweights of work and love.

Leadership is characterized by those who are "over you in the Lord." Again, the phrase describes function rather than position. The same Greek word was used in Romans 12:8 to describe those who lead. "In the Lord" emphasizes spiritual authority rather than power or decision-making authority. This phrase provides a clue about leadership authority in the New Testament. When we walk into the sphere of church life, we move out of the world of external authority and into the world of internal authority. We cannot settle for less, although there are many temptations to settle for authority as society knows it.

Inner authority comes from being in touch with our own experiences, as they ring true with biblical faith. This is different from ideas and opinions of others, no matter how powerful and influential are those expressing them. Communities of faith must foster in its members this inner authority where the law is not written in stone but is written on our hearts. This inner authority is tested and is confirmed by the testimony of the Holy Spirit. External authority vested in another or several "anothers" is quickly grabbed because we do not follow true biblical obedience and faith.

Inner authority brings both power and choice. The authority of others in our lives only works as we choose to give it. Never can it be imposed without choice. Choosing to give up power when we have none is meaningless. Giving others authority over us is purposeful only when we give up something important and when we are painfully aware that we have chosen to give it up. Authority in the Lord is chosen for spiritual good (2 Cor. 10:8) and is not the same as Jesus' warning of lording over them (Luke 22:25).

"Admonish" comes closest to our contemporary word *confront*. It literally means to "put into the mind" of another the claims of God on our lives. Confrontation plus care equals growth. Growth is limited without confrontation.

Paul used several words for confrontation—encourage, admonish, exhort, strengthen. They all point to a markedly aggressive approach to people rather than "just letting things be." Loving confrontation is a difficult yet needed aspect in any growing relationship. I cannot say that I have been successful at it. The loving commitment to another must be felt strongly for it to work. Confrontation is often seen as a push; and when we are pushed, we have a tendency to dig in our heels and push back.

Confrontation requires constant observation of the effect. There are no mechanical rules for it, and in many ways it pictures and expresses the whole complex relationship among people. Any two people may have entirely opposite reactions.

Confrontation is the exercise of power with humility and love. Power is the attempt to influence the course of a person's life. When we confront, we want to change the course of the way a person lives. Many people confront in subtle ways—suggestion, parables, reorganization, asking questions. We are usually left with the question, I wonder what that was all about? Biblical confrontation is more direct. It is making "I" statements rather than "you" statements. Confrontation is taking responsibility for my own feelings in a situation. "When you do this, I feel this way" may be a good way to initiate loving confrontation.

"Encourage" is another word that Paul used. Encouragement is not reassurance. When we tell others that things are going to get better, we are often heading for disillusionment. We do not know what the future holds. Things may get worse. Encouragement is not making predictions about the situation. This interpersonal skill seeks to provide heart, fortify the inner life, and strengthen the resources.

Encouragement calls for risk. People often lack the courage to try new things and face the risks involved. Most situations are not simple either/or situations. They involve some stretching of old patterns and trying out new patterns. That's risky. But it is also growth producing. Often the most helpful thing we can do for others is to help them face the risks squarely. For Paul, teaching and admonition went together. Both are necessary in bringing people to maturity in Christ (Col. 1:28). He challenged the Colossian Christians that the word of Christ would dwell in them richly as they "teach and admonish one another" (3:16). New principles are "put in the mind" with a view of changing behavior. This is an essential part of the learning process. It carries the idea of both correcting and confronting.

Confrontation works best in the natural, daily flow of interaction between people. Again, informality is the key. I have been told that I am a confrontive person. Some have said that my idea of a good meeting is to get people in a room, lock the door, and make them mad. It works when it is a part of the normal flow of communication and when it is mixed with trust, humor, and spontaneity. It points to the remarkable freedom of relationships between Christians. When it is part of the natural flow of interaction among people, the context and atmosphere it sets is helpful in more difficult, sticky, and corrective situations.

Whereas admonition is addressed to the mind or "putting sense into their heads," exhortation addresses the will and emotions. Exhortation is closely related to encouragement. Exhortation is a gift of the church to deal with apathy and indifference. The root meaning of the word is to call forth or to address. It can be translated *urge, entreat, beseech, encourage*. It is to be used to attack complacency, stagnation, and inertia. Exhortation defies the tendency to "settle in," to find normalcy in church life. The writer of Hebrews said, "Exhort one another every day, . . . that none of you may be hardened by the deceitfulness of sin" (3:13). Exhortation will call us together and challenge (stir up) us to live holy lives of love and good works (Heb. 10:24-27). The Greek word for "stir up" means to incite or irritate. It is the same word used in Acts 15:39 of a sharp contention between Paul and Barnabas.

The Greek word for "exhort" is the same word used for "comfort" in 1 Thessalonians 4:18. Again, it implies a speech that touches people deeply, probably a sharing of one's own inner life and struggle. When I am able to speak out of my own heart, from the depths of my own wounds, I am able to touch the wounds of others. Comfort is related to affliction, to the "press" of trouble, and originally comes from God, "the Father of mercies and God of all comfort, who comforts us in all our affliction, so that we may be able to comfort those who are in any affliction, with the comfort with which we ourselves are comforted by God" (2 Cor. 1:3). Those who help the hurting are those who are hurting themselves.

Love Them (5:13). Paul said the Thessalonians were to love those who were "over [them] in the Lord." Love can only be true of a relationship that is mutual. There may be respect in an over-under relationship but not love. Love takes priority over all leadership styles. Paul urged that those who lead be held in special esteem and affection. His adverb "exceedingly high" is expressive and in this precise form is found only here in the New Testament. Love should be the characteristic attitude of people in the church and is characteristic of relationships that are informal and close. This is not a matter of personal liking. It is not a matter of personalities. It is for the good of the church—"for their work's sake" (KJV). Love makes it possible for grace to be found among ourselves.

I remember telling a church leader that he was surrounded by people who would respect and follow him but who would not love him. He did not like it, but from my perspective it was true. Leaders who are not loved exact a heavy price. For they must lead from positional authority, guilt, and law. And the free-flowing momentum that comes only from love is lost down the drain of demand.

The issue of living at peace with strength is always an under-the-table issue in church life. It is difficult to live peacefully and significantly with strong people of both sexes. The crisis in church life in the years to come is finding ways of helping strong men and strong women relate well together in leadership positions.

The principles set forth in this Scripture passage admonish us to know and to love those who lead. Leadership calls for a combination of affection and respect. Affection and respect are two different ways of liking someone. A man can like a woman because of the way she relates to him personally. She is liked if she is kind and winsome and if he experiences a feeling of emotional warmth and closeness for her (affection). Or he can like her because of her ability outside their personal relationship (respect). Often when women try to lead, to achieve respect rather than to be liked, they attract a great deal of hostility. The best leaders receive both respect and affection, the combined aspects of liking.

The Weak (5:14)

The Bible tells the story of weak people and strong people. It talks about weak people becoming strong. There are sick people who are healed, people hurt by life who regain courage, timid and cowardly people who become powerful.

But there is also a cross. There is Christ in agony in the face of death and seemingly defeated to the point of believing himself forsaken by God. There is the great weakness of the disciples in the face of testing. Somewhere in all of this we find ourselves—sometimes strong and sometimes weak. The weak often give a powerful witness to a faith that frees them from weakness. Faith is a powerful freeing force. Someone has said that the Christian faith frees a person to fly like a glider if rising currents can be found. Faith is a rising current capable of bearing up our heavy burdens.

At the same time, it is hard for the healthy to understand the sick and the strong to understand the weak. We often are afraid that our weaknesses are something that other people don't have. But it is precisely at this point that we discover our freedom. At the spiritual level, we find that the ground is level—all are sinners, all are weak. In discovering our weaknesses, we find that we can be strong at one time and weak at another. We have strength to confess our weaknesses and to invest our strengths. Often natural strength is used to hide weakness. But spiritual strength frees us to acknowledge the power of our weaknesses.

Open the Bible and this is what you see—a toughness with the strong, the powerful, the virtuous, the rich, and the great. For it is often these good characteristics that keep people from God. With the weak, the poor, and the disabled, there is a profound tenderness and encouragement. The spiritual strength found in weakness frees us to bless others.

Jesus upset the apple cart when it came to strength and weakness. He was totally free to deal with people in new ways. However close our fellowship is with him, we never succeed in being as free as he was in relationships with the strong or the weak. Jesus shares our weaknesses and our strengths. He is neither strong nor weak in our meaning of those terms.

The New Testament church saw early in its life both the strong and the weak. Paul saw both clearly in the Thessalonian church. He talked about relationships with the strong. Principles for relating to the weak are given in 5:14.

"*Admonish the Idlers.*" The church will always have those who have no order in their lives. Apparently there were those in the church who felt the need to live on a constant "high." They were so emotionally excitable that they were unruly, living without concern for the church as a whole. Finally, they broke out into open rebellion. "Unruly" (KJV) really means those soldiers who got out of step with the ranks. They were to be warned of the consequences of their actions.

The church is seen as a disciplined group who are capable of marching together in close ranks. The disorderly or unruly are out of step or at least their discipline is slovenly and careless. Paul saw the importance of responsible disciplined work in the church. Duties are not to be neglected; excitement does not take the place of filling important responsibilities. Undisciplined living leads to carelessness with one's own life and with the lives of others. Carelessness brings idleness and an appearance of concern for others which includes busybodyness. We cannot live off of excitement. The intoxication of continual excitement leads to fanaticism, meddling in the lives of others, and the constant search for a new spiritual "highs."

"Encourage the Fainthearted." We are to give heart to those people who lack courage. Fear brings its own special kind of bondage. "Fainthearted" describes those who are broken in spirit and who have lost confidence in themselves and their abilities. "Encourage" means to attach ourselves to them, to cling to them. The world despises people for cowardice. But the church has always been willing to protect those who are weak and depressed.

Depression often comes from inadequate or defensive attempts to cope with unmet personal needs and expectations. Discouragement carries the idea of being "broken in spirit," completely disillusioned about oneself, and having no inward sense of personal worth. Faintheartedness comes from that kind of deflated feeling of worthlessness. Encouragement fortifies, gives heart, brings back strengths.

"Help the Weak." Third, we are to help and to support the weak. The reference points to those who are weak spiritually. Spiritual weakness is seen in an inability to face what each day has to bring. The weak need to feel that they are not alone as they face life. We are to cling to the weak ones and make sure they do not feel abandoned. By clinging to them, we help them to stand firm. The strong are to support (KJV) and "hold fast" the weak. "Strengthen the weak hands,/and make firm the feeble knees./ Say to those who are of a fearful heart,/Be strong, fear not!" (Isa. 35:3-4). Clinging (translated *help*) is the same word that is used in Matthew 6:24 and Luke 16:13 of clinging to one master.

When I first began studying this verse, I identified with the helper rather than with the helped. But I have discovered the faintheartedness of weakness, the loss of nerve, the feeling that the reservoirs of courage have all run out. Many people who are used to being strong are very hesitant to confess need. To know that others are there and can be held on to is a buttress in life that everyone needs. This helping, clinging, implies an interpersonal closeness that is expressed through affection, loyalty, and simple practical deeds of helpfulness.

"Be Patient with Them All." Finally, we are to be patient with all. This calls for steadfast, active perseverance. At no time do we forsake them. This patience with our fellow Christians is a unique gift. Christian growth is often a plan of slow development. There are old natures, old habits, old

circumstances to be dealt with. Be content to wait. When we learn to be patient, we also learn to cover, to forget, and to overlook many faults in others. When we cannot be patient, we carry with us something which cannot be overlooked, and it begins to wrinkle and warp inside. Only true patience covers; everything else is but a cover-up.

To whom are these words addressed? The letter is to the whole church. This ministry of warnings and encouragement is the mutual responsibility of all church members. All have moments when we feel strong. Certainly all experience times of weakness.

Patience is demanded when we work closely with people. Closeness with people creates injuries and irritations. There is no closeness without friction. It is part of the package that is wrapped up in relationships. God is patient with us. He bides his time, refusing to be offended, waiting for us to grow up.

Henri Nouwen's image of the wounded healer is a model of the church's ministry to the weak. The man sits at the city gate with the other sick and diseased. His wounds are just as deep; his suffering is just as severe as others who live the life of hurt. But he takes time out from dressing his own wounds to clean and bandage the wounds of others.

Paul saw that we are all in need of help and are all able to give help. He saw it because he was aware of the human situation. He was never fooled by human depravity, but he was also conscious of the power of the gospel as dynamite in human lives. It transformed dead people into live people, weak people into powerful people, and empty people longing for significance into deeply fulfilled people who found meaning out of both their strengths and weaknesses.

Developing Spontaneity in Relationships (5:15-22)

Paul continued this remarkable manifesto of freedom with simple exhortation toward spontaneity in relationships. The happiest relationships are spontaneous, freely given, without constraint or effort. In comfortable relationships, we are free from self-consciousness. Things happen without planning or premeditation. We can be talkative or silent, profound or mundane, serious or funny. Any way is all right. Being together is enough.

Urging people to be spontaneous is like urging them to be happy. The harder we try, the more we fail. Spontaneity is a by-product of other things going on in Christians' lives. But it renews our lives like free-flowing springs, providing both refreshment and vigor.

The first qualities that feed the springs of spontaneity are love and devotion. I have a very simple theory of motivation. Love motivates. The power to do comes from love. Love makes us bold, ardent, enthusiastic, and sometimes, impulsive. Love fills up the heart and spills over into all kinds of surprising behavior.

The next characteristic of spontaneity is freedom. The spontaneous person is uncomfortable with locked-in methods and procedures. People who are free know more ways of doing good than one. They do not ask beforehand. They trust their judgment that the spontaneous thing will be appropriate and meaningful.

The touching story of the anointing of Jesus by Mary at Bethany reveals the true spirit of spontaneity. Mary is the model of the qualities of devotion and freedom—loving ardently and extravagantly, fearlessly and originally. The anointing of Jesus was the natural thing to do; easier to do than not to do. Like the disciples, we don't know what to do with Mary's free spirit. But Jesus intimated that what she had done would be a model for Christian spontaneity in relationships (Mark 14:9).

What is life without spontaneity? At the extremes, we experience ourselves as an assembling of mechanical parts. A boy named Joey pictures the tragic loss of inner freedom.

Joey functioned as if run by machines or remote control. Not only did he believe that he was a machine but, more remarkably, he also created this impression in others. You see, Joey was a schizophrenic fifteen-year-old who chose the machine and froze himself in its image. His was the fierce and unconscious rejection of the human world which had apparently rejected him. When he entered the dining room at the hospital, he would string an imaginary wire to his chair or table from an equally imaginary electric outlet. He then carefully plugged himself in. Only then, with the current turned on, could Joey eat or show any signs of life.

What is especially striking about Joey is that his actions convinced doctors and others around him to respond to him as a machine rather than as a human being. For example, they were careful not to step on his "wires" and failed even to notice him during the long silent intervals when he was "turned off." It was not Joey alone who believed in this mechanical nature. He also made believers of those who encountered him. By living his illusion, Joey made it real to himself and to others.

Joey is a flesh-and-blood example of living in bondage. He was programmed to tight inner controls. He was barricaded, boxed in, and insulated from the loving influences of other people. Every nerve, impulse, thought, and feeling was wired to be mechanical. It's a long way from Joey to the glorious liberty of the children of God (Rom. 8:21).

For the Christian, freedom is found only in the grace of God. Jesus Christ, the only truly free person, found his freedom in being devoted to the Father. The nearer we are to the Father the more freedom we experience.

A friend of mine has a small plaque above his desk. It is a paraphrase of 1 Thessalonians 5:16-18:

> Rejoice always,
> Pray without ceasing,
> In everything give thanks;
> For this is the will of God in
> Christ Jesus to you.

Only a free person can want or do this. A person who desires these goals is not locked into a pattern. These are the characteristics of a spontaneous faith, fed by the inner springs of devotion and freedom.

The last part of 1 Thessalonians 5:18 is the core of truth that unlocks these springs for us so they can flow in our lives: "for this is the will of God in Christ Jesus for you." In other words, the secret to finding the life-giving forces comes from the will of God through Christ Jesus. We are free because God wills it. Freedom comes through that marvelous grace "in Jesus Christ." The will of God is revealed in Jesus. In him we are given the power to truly love according to that will.

Freedom (5:15-18)

Free to Do Good (5:15). Freedom comes from following that which is good. In the context of the verse, good stands against evil. This is not to be understood as small acts of kindness but of lives lived in an attitude of Christian love. All of our lives, we are to follow continually after those things that bring good to others. Paul was saying, in effect, "When you have been wronged, be free enough not to retaliate." He saw that doing good was a corporate responsibility. The whole group is held responsible for the conduct of each person. All of you see that none of you retaliate.

But Paul was not simply saying that we should do little deeds of love when we might be expected to retaliate. He was setting down goodness as a principle of life. It is one of those springs of action that keeps life fresh and spontaneous. Pursue the good with great eagerness. Loving others is good for us and good for them. When we are part of the good things that happen to others, we find that those same things are good for us.

Free to Rejoice (5:16). Rejoicing is a challenge to welcome all of life with expectancy. We can tackle all that life offers and come back for more. This calls for a profound trust that God can use everything for our good. Paul had learned that affliction and deep joy may go together (2 Cor. 6:10). The Bible often couples joy with trouble and tribulation. In Romans 12:11-12, Paul said that we should not try to slip out from under it or try to evade it: "Be patient in tribulation." The early church expected trouble and usually got it. The scars trouble left were considered metals of honor, given by the Lord's own hands. But what the early Christians received from trouble was not what the world expected. They received "glad tidings of great joy."

As a child of the Heavenly Father, the Christian goes rejoicing through the Father's world, gladly living out the implications of faith. The spontaneous way of the Christian is a happy way. We are free to have songs in our hearts, and those songs come from being "in Christ."

The word *joy* occurs with startling frequency in the New Testament. New Testament faith is permeated with this spirit of holy joy. When we tie the word "rejoice" to 1 Thessalonians 5:15, we find one of the secrets to joy. On all occasions, seek to bring good to someone, and then on all occasions we will have joy. Paul knew what it was to rejoice in difficult circumstances (Acts 16:25) so he could say, "Rejoice always." When we have that "joy unspeakable and full of glory" (1 Pet. 1:8, KJV), the bubbling springs take over. Who knows what will happen!

Free to Pray (5:17). To speak the language of prayer is to speak the language of love. How is your love life? That will say something about your prayer life. How intimate are your conversations with others? That will say something about your willingness to open your heart to God. Prayer is a dialogue between two who love each other because prayer is the language of the heart. Prayer is saying what the heart wants to say. When we hear the admonition to pray constantly, we are being taught to be in a constant state of conversation with God.

Prayer was as natural to Paul as breathing. At anytime he was likely to break off a discussion or to sum it up by some great prayer. In the same way, our lives can be lived in such an attitude of dependence on God that we will easily and naturally move into words of prayer. Ephesians 6:18 says, "Pray at all times"; Romans 12:12, "be constant in prayer"; Luke 18:1, pray "always." All of these have the same meaning. We are to always be ready to turn to God in worshipful ways. The heart that is "tuned in" to God turns to God in secret thoughts as well as in outward actions.

Prayer and joy are connected in our lives like they are connected in 1 Thessalonians 5:16-17. In prayer we find the ways to remove that which has blocked the joy. Without prayer, the springs quit bubbling and stagnate. Our lives are blocked by the collection of garbage in our souls. Things go sour. We collect things rather than pray about them. When we are in persistent conversation with God, we are able to deal with our feelings immediately. We don't have to pollute the springs of spontaneity with unresolved attitudes and feelings. We can verbalize them immediately to God. That's why it is important to pray without ceasing.

Outside the New Testament, the words *without ceasing* describe a hacking cough. The person with a hacking cough is not always audibly coughing, but the tendency to cough is always there. So the Christian who prays without ceasing is not always audibly praying; yet prayer is always the attitude of heart and life.

Free to Give Thanks (5:18). We all need to know that what we have are gifts from God. Often our successes block off the inner springs more than our failures or problems do. We get satisfied. We begin to think that we have accomplished something. We try to latch onto it and make sure it doesn't escape. We take the credit for what we have obtained. We need to be reminded that it all comes from God.

Many do not find the secret of thanksgiving. Some meet life with some things that make them happy and other things about which they complain bitterly. We welcome those things which bring us good and complain about those things which do not. But when Christ comes into our lives, we see his purpose working out. That purpose is being worked out even in those events which we do not welcome. We learn to give thanks in all things.

The explanation for "all things" is found in Romans 8:28, "We know that all things work together for good to them that love God, to them who are the called according to his purpose" (KJV). This is the secret to Christian freedom. If everything works to do us good, how can we do otherwise than give thanks?

Devotion (5:19-22)

Devotion to the Spirit (5:19). The Holy Spirit brings enthusiasm and excitement to our lives. The Spirit makes us spontaneous. When we are spontaneous, we can look at life with the same wide-eyed excitement about new things that we had when we were much younger. We give ourselves chances to get excited about the things we do.

Let's hear it for those with enthusiasm! For their faith flames up quite hot. Enthusiasm is often translated "aglow" or "fervent." In Romans 12:11 it literally means to "boil over." The Spirit brings enthusiasm, a total and complete abandonment for what one is doing. The feeling is there. Without the feeling, our lives are like unlighted candles or a fire of green wood; there is plenty of smoke, but no flame.

The fire of the Holy Spirit melts the coldness in our hearts. The cold creates fear, and fear causes calculation and speculation. Trying to figure everything out jams up the flow of spontaneity. The warmth of the Spirit melts the desire to be shrewd and cunning (the opposite of spontaneity). We don't have to add everything up before we act. We can throw away the calculators. Paul was saying not to pour cold water on the Holy Spirit's urgings. One sure sign of the Holy Spirit's work in our lives is our ability to give ourselves unreservedly to what we are doing. We don't hold back. The kids have a good way of saying it, "We go with the flow." Without the Holy Spirit, the Christian life would lack all notions of spontaneity.

Devotion to the Truth (5:20). The prophet spoke because of a "revelation" (1 Cor. 14:30). From the human standpoint, this truth might be like a "shot out of the blue." If there are prophets among us, we are always in for surprises. Since God has spoken through people in this way, the spontaneous was always possible.

Prophets are compelled to speak God's message. The prophet may think: *I can't say that. If I let what I'm thinking out of my mouth, it will cause all kinds of trouble. People won't understand.* But the truth comes out. The word of God is declared spontaneously. The prophets love the truth because the truth is from God.

The principle for our lives today is similar to the way God worked with the prophets of old. The prophet was always ready for new truth. He or she was always willing to keep on learning. Paul gave a helpful definition of prophesy. "One who prophesies, preaching the messages of God, is helping others grow in the Lord, encouraging and comforting them (1 Cor. 14:3, TLB). In Joel 2:28-29, we encounter the promise that the prophetic spirit would be given both to the sons and daughters of God. Peter saw the beginning of that fulfillment on the Day of Pentecost when he said, "Your young men shall see visions, and your old men shall dream dreams; yea, and on my menservants and my maidservants in those days I will pour out my spirit; and they shall prophesy" (Acts 2:16-18).

God will give us the ability to speak for truth. When we have something to say, it's important to say it. God has gifted us with the remarkable ability to tell others what he is saying to us. Don't hold back, and don't despise prophesying!

Devotion to the Real (5:21-22). Another spring that gives our lives verve and vigor is spiritual discernment. Paul was saying to find out the spiritual value of everything, and either hold fast to it or hold aloof from it. The word "test" or "prove" (KJV) is often used in testing metals or checking out budgets. "Prove all things" (KJV) refers to the process of sifting out the genuine from the counterfeit. Paul was not saying to try everything once. He was saying that we should test everything that represents itself as good. The good should be accepted. Every kind of evil should be avoided.

There is a spiritual chemistry in proving that makes the true and authentic come to the surface. The call of Jesus to "come and see" says that everything must be tested through personal values and experiences and must be tried and examined well before making a final choice.

Once we have tested everything, the practical rule applies: hold onto the good; hold off the evil. The Thessalonians were asked to apply tests. There are things that appear on the surface to be good. There are some things that are claimed to be from God. They are not simply to be accepted at face value. Although we are to approach life simply, we are not to approach it naively. All things must be tested. Two strong words are used here. "Hold fast" denotes the firm acceptance of the good. It emphasizes acceptance and belonging. "Abstain" (KJV) is a strong word also. It emphasizes rejection and separation. If a thing is evil, the believer must have no trust in it whatever.

The springs of freedom and devotion are ways we keep in touch with those inner urgings of the Holy Spirit. We don't have to go looking for them. They are no further from us than our fingers are from our hands. If we try to ignore them, we lose the spontaneity that God intended for us daily. If we "go with the flow," we find rivers of living water that spring up to eternal life.

6
The Language of Blessing
5:23-28

The Bible carries through its pages two strong themes: deliverance, or the saving acts of God, and blessing, or the gracious abiding presence of God. Deliverance brings salvation which proclaims the saving acts of God in specific events. Blessing brings the gracious abiding presence of God which upholds, sustains, and undergirds all of life. Blessing is that overabundance of the graciousness of God in the daily events of life.

Deliverance and blessing are experienced differently. Deliverance is experienced in events that represent God's intervention. He moves into our lives and changes things. Blessing is the continuing activity of God in daily experience. Deliverance has to do with redemption and liberation and rescue. Blessing has to do with care, nurture, and sustenance.

When Paul came to a benediction, he used the language of blessing. A benediction is an expression of the grace of God in the ordinariness of life. Paul imparted a blessing, an act of bestowing wholeness, intactness, health, and well-being. God's blessing causes growth, maturation, prospering, and increase. The life cycle of people cannot be understood apart from blessing. Blessing is inclusive of everything in life—freedom from danger, security, good fortune, and well-being.

The act of blessing is one of the most intimate interpersonal transactions. The Old Testament concept of blessing imparted a vital power to another person. The one who blesses gives the other person something of one's own soul. When friends part, they bless each other to bind the relationship. Significant interpersonal life is impossible without blessing. When the inner lives of people meet, they bless one another. This blessing either brings out or renews spiritual community. For blessing to be meaningful, it must be reciprocal, giving the power of life and the intensification of life to one another.

At the end of this letter, Paul wanted to give the Thessalonians something. He wanted good for them, so he blessed them. Blessing is poured out on others with power-laden words. When it is spoken, it contains a deep reality. In our world, hellos and good-byes may have little meaning; but if the hellos and good-byes disappearerd, a part of the richness of interpersonal life would disappear. Blessing is the verbalization of meaningful hellos and good-byes. So it is important that we look at the beautiful language of blessing in all its aspects.

Blessing contains both words and actions. The words of blessing are found in 1 Thessalonians 5:23-24. The actions of blessing are found in 1 Thessalonians 5:25-27.

The Words of Blessing (5:23-24)

The exhortations were concluded, and Paul passed on to a prayer for his readers. The prayer was directed to the God of peace. Peace brings about prosperity in the widest sense, especially spiritual prosperity. This is the same theme that is found in 1 Thessalonians 1:1.

Wholeness (5:23)

Paul used an interesting compound word in speaking of wholeness. "May the God of peace himself sanctify you wholly" (v. 23). Both words mean to be whole. Paul was saying, in effect, "May God make each one of you whole through and through, every part of you." "Sanctify you wholly" suggests finality as well as completeness. Paul's prayer was that his friends would be held intact in the whole of their personal lives. This prayer should put to rest any ideas of the separation between spirit, soul, and body. The whole person is preserved. Each is to reach the end for which one was made. Completeness implies the unity of spirit, soul, and body.

Preservation (5:23)

Paul's prayer was that the whole person be preserved entire and without blame. All of our powers are to be committed and set apart for God. This totality is brought out in the verb translated "kept" or

"preserved" (KJV) and the adjective translated "sound" or "whole" (KJV).
One word carries the thought of "that which has attained its end" and the
other "that which is complete in all its parts."

Presence (5:23-24)

It is typical of this letter that wholeness and preservation should be
followed by "at the coming of our Lord Jesus Christ." The presence of
Christ in the midst of his people becomes the final word, and it places a
new emphasis on the wholeness of people. Paul was not thinking of a
sanctification that might last for a little time here on earth; he was
thinking of one that continues at the coming of Christ. We will be in the
process of becoming whole at his coming.

God will cause it to happen! The word goes forth and accomplishes
its promise through action. God doesn't just call us. He also will empower
us to do what he is calling us to do. The effect of this is to emphasize the
doing, to fasten attention on the fact that God will bring to pass what he
has begun. This moves us from the words of blessing to the actions of
blessing.

The Actions of Blessing (5:25-27)

The actions of blessing are suggested through three very concrete
expressions: prayer, the holy kiss, and the reading of Scripture.

The Prayer for Others (5:25)

I think in this verse Paul revealed his uncertainty and weakness. He
found himself in situations where he did not know how to act. He
struggled as his friends struggled. When he did act, he was not at all sure
that he had done the right thing. So again he used the affectionate address
"brethren" with the request that they continually pray for him. This
request for prayer emphasizes the reciprocal need between Paul and his
Thessalonian friends.

In intercessory prayer, we experience both the companionship of God
and of other persons. Praying for others wraps us all up together in the
presence of the Father. This is especially true if we pray audibly for others
in their presence. If such prayer brings the blessings of God, why don't we

wrap ourselves in it more often? Do we not believe in the power of intercessory prayer? Or are we frightened by the interpersonal vulnerability and intimacy that results?

The Holy Kiss (5:26)

The holy kiss was a public demonstration of affection between Christians. It is mentioned in Romans 16:16; 1 Corinthians 16:20; 2 Corinthians 13:12; and as "the kiss of love" in 1 Peter 5:14. Apparently the custom was widely practiced in New Testament days. An interesting comment from the early worship of the church is found in the *Constitutions* of the *Holy Apostles* about the third century AD.

> In like manner, let the deacon watch the people, that no body whispers or sleeps or laughs or nods. . . . After this let all arise together, and looking toward the east . . . pray to God eastward. . . . After the prayer is over, let some of the deacons attend upon the oblation of the Eucharist. . . . Let other deacons watch the multitude and keep them silent. But let that deacon who is at the high-priest's right hand say to the people, "Let no one have any dispute with another, let no one come in hypocrisy." Then let the men give the men, and the women give the women, the Lord's kiss.

In time it became the custom for the kiss to be exchanged between men and women. Clement of Alexandria had apprehensions about the kissing custom. He complained: "There are those that do nothing but make the churches resound with kisses." Abuses of this kind led to restriction of the custom. There are several regulations dealing with the custom in the early church councils.

I think Paul was free in his expression of affection. He was saying, "Give all the brethren a kiss for me." Picture it. After reading the letter did everyone go around kissing others? Probably so. Isn't it great! Obviously the expressions of affection were demonstrated in the New Testament with much less reserve than is observed today. In a way it is a visible expression of a church's interpersonal richness—visible, vulnerable, nurturing, and spontaneous. A church that kisses well loves well.

The Old Testament pictures kissing as a way of communicating forgiveness. In the story of Esau and Jacob, reconciliation took place after twenty years of separation. "Esau ran to meet him, and embraced him, and fell on his neck and kissed him, and they wept" (Gen. 33:4). Joseph accepted his older brothers who had sold him into slavery in this manner. "He kissed all his brothers and wept upon them; and after that his brothers talked with him" (Gen. 45:15). This Old Testament emphasis on the kiss was continued in the New Testament. Jesus endorsed the kiss of hospitality and was warmly appreciative of the one who kissed his feet thoroughly (Luke 7:44-48). The most famous kiss in the New Testament is the kiss of Judas. It was also the most blatant and the most damaging.

Kisses are "holy" when they are exchanged between those holy and separated ones. It is a natural symbol of the intense family affection in the church. In AD 200, Tertullian indicated that the congregational prayers were concluded with the kiss. Cyril of Jerusalem said that the kiss was a sign of peace and concord in the church. "This kiss is the sign that our souls are united, and that we banish all remembrance of injury." However, over a period of four centuries, the church had exchanged its attitude of emotional expression to an attitude of emotional suppression.

For several years I worked in a church with a large number of senior adults. They are great kissers! I guess they needed to kiss, and I am one who needs to be kissed. Hardly a Sunday went by that I didn't receive a big one, and the more they resounded, the better. They blessed my life. A church leader was once asked how he got away with hugging all the women. He responded, "That's it, I hug *all* the women." This public expression of affection through hugs and kisses is a natural response of Christians in community.

The Reading of Scripture (5:27)

Paul used strong language in wanting this Scripture to be read before the whole church. The word "read" here means to be read aloud. It is not likely that all of the church members of Thessalonica could read. Reading aloud was the only way the contents of the letter could be made known to all. The reading of Scripture brings blessing, and Paul "puts them on oath" that they would be sure to read the letter to all. This fits with Paul's strong expressions of affection and his desire to be with them again. He wanted to make sure that all would hear the words of his letter. In ideal circumstances, Paul would have returned to them. Since he could not see them "face-to-face," it was important that all heard the words of the letter. In this way, his care for them would be manifested.

Grace to You (5:28)

We stop where we began, with grace. The first word and the last word of the Christian's interpersonal life is grace to you! Paul had nowhere else to go. He was the "apostle of the heart set free." He knew from experience that "where the Spirit of the Lord is, there is freedom" (2 Cor. 3:17).

No matter where Paul's writings lead us, they begin and end with grace. Our capacities for learning and loving are nurtured through significant people and through a work of power breaking in through the grace of God. Grace comes through conscious and unconscious ways, through loving persons, through intimacy with Holy Scripture, and through ways we may never understand. Learning that transforms does not bring grace, but recognizes those gifts when they come.

Grace also brings us to that terrifying moment of freedom and the immediate impulse to push it away. Wasn't I more secure with the feeling that someone was keeping the balance sheets and the scorecard? What do I do now? Lord, give me grace to overcome my fear of grace.

> 'Twas grace that taught my heart to fear,
> And grace my fears relieved;

It is through grace that we survive trauma. Grace seeks us and won't let us go. But there are traps along the way if we are too ardent in our seeking. More often than not, we stumble upon it, like a treasure in the field. There is nothing we can do to bring this marvelous grace of our loving Lord. We live under his eyes, at the center of his vision. And those eyes are loving eyes, "like a [mother] taking care of her children" (1 Thess. 2:7).

> 'Tis grace hath bro't me safe thus far,
> And grace will lead me home.

Appendix

What kind of learning process provides the best environment for transformation? I do not know nor does anyone else. But I venture to say that it is some kind of interaction between personal experience and the biblical text with time for reflection and time for application in specific life situations. I say that, knowing that the work of God's grace transcends both our understanding of content and process. But if I could put the work of grace in a learning framework, this is the pattern I would use.

Some may be interested in the more theoretical aspects of learning cycles. In spite of different labels, most learning-cycle theorists use concepts to describe how people learn and ultimately manifest a change in behavior![1] Jones and Pfeiffer have developed an experiential learning cycle of experiencing (activity), publishing (sharing reactions), processing (patterns and dynamics), generalizing (principles), and applying (planning).[2] Kolb, Rubin, and McIntyre designed a learning model around concrete experiences (demands of the real world) and observation or reflection on experience. This leads to the formulation of abstract concepts and application or "testing concepts in new situations." The learning inventory in this appendix is an adaptation of a learning-style inventory from Kolb, Rubin, and McIntyre.[3]

James and Evelyn Whitehead developed a model for theological reflection in ministry.[4] Their model points to three sources of information that are important in personal decision making: Christian tradition (Scripture and church history), personal experience (individual believer and the community of faith), and cultural information (social sciences and other disciplines). This model suggests that these resources are all available in helping persons respond faithfully to personal needs.

James E. Loder has developed five steps that are descriptive of a transforming event.[5] The first step is a "rupture" in what is known which creates an inner conflict and a need to set things right. The second step is an interlude for scanning—a time of waiting and wondering, looking over the terrain of one's situation and searching out possible solutions. The third step is the constructive act of imagination—an insight, intuition, or vision, which impacts with convincing force and leads to the transformation of the ruptured situation. The fourth step is characterized by release and openness—a release of energy that has been "bound up" and a freedom to move in new directions. There is a "sigh of relief" which often brings a wave of new insights. The final step is an interpretation of the solution into behavior that is a gain over the original conditions. In summary, transformational knowing is carried on conjointly as imagination and personal intuitions interact with reflective or theoretical knowledge.[6]

All the models suggest that we are stronger in some of these processes and weaker in others. Personal learning styles are like different channels on our television sets. We naturally shift to those channels that come in clearer and quickly move past those channels that are fuzzy and out of focus.

There is also the suggestion that skills in all phases of the learning cycle are required for effective learning. Therefore, learning is moving through a series of steps, although these steps may not be followed in any sequence. However, each step must eventually occur if the learning process is to be complete.

The process is complex. No one goes through the process clean—it's hop-step all the way. The vertical line on Figure 1 represents the individual, systematic, ordered, coherent "organizing" of life. It is willful and powerful, always wanting to take over, without knowing that destroying the balance sabotages the whole. The vertical line seeks balance and wholeness. It represents the relational, unpredictable, spontaneous "bursting" of life. Transformation comes in the blending of both parts and whole.

What happens when all the parts come together in the study of the Bible? I can only venture a guess. Learning is a thinking, feeling process of bringing our whole selves to the biblical text. When the thinking, choosing, rational process connects with the intuitive, emotional, and relational process, the sparks are ignited. We transcend the ordinary. Through the power of the Holy Spirit, we experience revelation and are changed (transformed). We test both our experience of Scripture and our interpretation of Scripture in Christ's body, the church, waiting for some confirmation that "it has seemed good to the Holy Spirit and to us" (Acts 15:28).

Learning Inventory

Instructions

This inventory is designed to help you understand your method of learning or way of knowing. Give a high rank to words that best characterize the way you know and a low rank to words that least characterize your learning style. The aim of the inventory is to locate your primary ways of knowing and learning, not to evaluate your ability.

There are ten sets of four words. Rank order each set of four words (horizontally), assigning a 4 to the word that best characterizes your learning style, a 3 to the word that next best characterizes your learning style, a 2 to the next most characteristic of you as a learner, and a 1 to the word that is least characteristic of you as a learner. Be sure to assign a different rank number to each of the four words. Total your scores (vertically) at the bottom of each column. Mark your scores on the vertical and horizontal lines of the diagram, with the center identified as zero and the outside circle as forty.

1. __personal	__analytical	__relational	__practical
2. __receptive	__discriminating	__intimate	__active
3. __sensing	__thinking	__feeling	__practicing
4. __accepting	__evaluative	__aware	__risk taking
5. __intuitive	__logical	__questioning	__productive
6. __concrete	__abstract	__subjective	__involved
7. __immediate	__informative	__reflective	__pragmatic
8. __experiential	__conceptual	__relevant	__experimental
9. __spontaneous	__rational	__intense	__responsible
10. __nonverbal	__verbal	__imaginative	__objective

Totals: _____ _____ _____ _____

     Experience   Exegesis   Reflection   Application

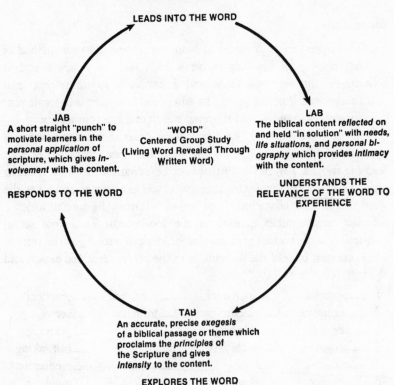

GRAB
A point of *interest* related to the learner's *experience,* yet expressed in an unusual way, which gives *immediacy* to the content.

LEADS INTO THE WORD

JAB
A short straight "punch" to motivate learners in the *personal application* of scripture, which gives *involvement* with the content.

"WORD"
Centered Group Study
(Living Word Revealed Through Written Word)

LAB
The biblical content *reflected* on and held "in solution" with *needs, life situations,* and *personal biography* which provides *intimacy* with the content.

RESPONDS TO THE WORD

UNDERSTANDS THE RELEVANCE OF THE WORD TO EXPERIENCE

TAB
An accurate, precise *exegesis* of a biblical passage or theme which proclaims the *principles* of the Scripture and gives *intensity* to the content.

EXPLORES THE WORD

Notes

INTRODUCTION
  1. James Smart, *The Strange Silence of the Bible in the Church* (Philadelphia: The Westminster Press, 1970), p. 15.
  2. Richard L. Rubenstein, *My Brother Paul* (New York: Harper & Row Publishers, Inc., 1972), p. 6.

CHAPTER 2
  1. Erik Erikson, *Young Man Luther* (New York: W. W. Norton and Co., 1958), p. 115.
  2. William Barclay, *New Testament Words* (Philadelphia: The Westminster Press, 1974), pp. 77-78.

CHAPTER 3
  1. H. P. Liddon, *Sermons on the Old Testament* (London, 1904). Quoted in Leon Morris, *The First and Second Epistles to the Thessalonians* (Grand Rapids: William B. Eerdman's Co., 1959), p. 105.

CHAPTER 4
  1. Quoted in *The Interpreter's Bible*, Volume 10 (Nashville: Abingdon Press, 1953), p. 319.
  2. Malcolm Muggeridge and Alec Vidler, *Paul: Envoy Extraordinary* (New York: Harper & Row, Publishers, Inc., 1972), p. 108.
  3. Oliver Wendell Holmes, "The Deacon's Masterpiece or, The Wonderful 'One-Hoss Shay,'" *The Complete Poetical Works of Oliver Wendell Holmes* (New York: Houghton Mifflin Co., 1908), p. 160.

APPENDIX
  1. Albert B. Palmer, "Learning Cycles: Models of Behavioral Change," J. E. Jones and J. W. Pfeiffer, eds., *The 1981 Annual Handbook for Group Facilitators* (San Diego: University Associates, 1981), pp. 147-153.
  2. John E. Jones and J. William Pfeiffer, *The 1975 Annual Handbook for Group Facilitators* (San Diego: University Associates, 1981), pp. 3-5.
  3. David A. Kolb, Irwin W. Ruben, and James M. McIntyre, *Organizational Pyschology: An Experiential Approach* (Englewood Cliffs: Prentice Hall, Inc., 1971), pp. 24-29.
  4. James and Evelyn Whitehead, *Method in Ministry* (New York: The Seabury Press, 1980), pp. 13-21.
  5. James E. Loder, *The Transforming Moment* (San Francisco: Harper & Row, Publishers, 1981), pp. 31-35.
  6. Ibid., p. 59.

Selected Bibliography

Barclay, William. *New Testament Words*. Philadelphia: The Westminster Press, 1974. Barclay has the unique gift of getting the most out of biblical images. He turns on the pictures in the head. With all the emphasis on "video," the pictures in the head are still the most interesting and the most dynamic.

Clarke, James W., and Bailey, John W. *The First and Second Epistles to The Thessalonians, (The Interpreter's Bible, Volume 11)*. Nashville: Abingdon Press, 1955. Exegesis and exposition on 1 Thessalonians. The writers see two great themes: the note of thanksgiving and the yearning and prayerful desire of Paul to see the Thessalonians abound more and more in grace.

Hendriksen, William. *New Testament Commentary. Exposition of I and II Thessalonians*. Grand Rapids: Baker Book House, 1955. Hendriksen calls 1 Thessalonians a letter of encouragement. "You're doing fine, continue to do so more and more."

Hobbs, Herschel H. *1-2 Thessalonians, (The Broadman Bible Commentary, Volume 2)*. Nashville: Broadman Press, 1971. "No matter how hard one's task may be, it is made lighter to know that others in similar circumstances are standing by the faith and are remembering other Christians in love and fellowship" (Commentary on 1 Thess. 3:8).

Howard, J. Grant. *The Trauma of Transparency: A Biblical Approach to Inter-Personal Communication*. Portland: Multnomah Press, 1979. The writer believes that there is a deep need in the Christian community for a theology of interpersonal communication. This book is a primer for Christians with good use of biblical principles.

Jordan, Clarence. *The Cotton Patch Version of Paul's Epistles*. New York: Association Press. Jordan knew intimately the language of the Bible and the language of the people. He was able to bridge the gap. "May the Lord load you up and run you over with love for one another and for everybody else too, the same as we have for you" (1 Thess. 3:12).

Kaiser, Walter C. *Toward an Exegetical Theology, Biblical Exegesis for Preaching and Teaching*. Grand Rapids: Baker Book House, 1981. The crises in biblical studies is in the discipline of exegesis. The biblical text should be the focus of attention for congregation and speaker. Instead it is buried under tradition, anecdotes and "faddish practical chatter." This book teaches the methods of exegesis.

Loder, James E. *The Transforming Moment Understanding Convictional Experiences*. San

Francisco: Harper and Row, Publishers, 1981. Loder draws on theology, psychology, philosophy, and learning theory to present a model of "convictional knowing"—those sudden life-changing bursts of religious experience. The convictional experience is the intimate face of the Holy which endures even through the fear of absorption or abandonment. That is an abstract but accurate description of my experience with 1 Thessalonians 2:7-8.

Morris, Leon. *The First and Second Epistles to the Thessalonians.* Grand Rapids: William B. Eerdmans Publishing Co., 1959. This commentary comes closest to catching the interpersonal theme of the letter. "The great thing was that he wrote in exultation of spirit, having just heard the good news of the way in which they were standing fast."

Ogilvie, Lloyd John. *Life as It Was Meant to Be.* Ventura: Regal Books, 1980. A good example of relating the text of the Thessalonian letters to the needs of the people.

Plummer, Alfred. *A Commentary on St. Paul's First Epistle to the Thessalonians.* London: Robert Scott, 1918. This old commentary was dug out of a library grave and is a prize. First Thessalonians is "simple and pure religion rather than reasoned and systematized theology."

Rubenstein, Richard L. *My Brother Paul.* New York: Harper & Row, Publishers, Inc., 1972. A fascinating study of Paul from the discipline of depth psychology. The writer expands on Paul's ability to use picture language and mental images. He sees Paul as both a visionary and an organizer, a mystic and an administrator.

Smart, James D. *The Strange Silence of the Bible in the Church.* Philadelphia: The Westminster Press, 1970. This book continues to speak to the great gulf fixed between the biblical analysis of the scholars and the biblical hunger of the people.

Whitehead, James D., and Eaton, Evelyn. *Method in Ministry.* New York: The Seabury Press, 1980. The task of reflection in ministry is "to recover and overcome"—recover the meanings and overcome the trappings. This book provides a good model for theological reflection.

Wink, Walter. *The Bible in Human Transformation.* Philadelphia: Fortress Press, 1973. Wink takes on traditional biblical scholarship and the historical critical method as incapable of evoking personal transformation. He sees exegesis in context and "communal exegesis" as the way a biblical text speaks to persons in a way that they must respond.

Wink, Walter. *Transforming Bible Study.* Nashville: Abingdon Press, 1980. A how-to book on Bible study, using the concepts of Carl Jung and brain hemisphere theory. Wink brings four disciples to this book: "a commitment to transformation, a love for the New Testament, a sense of the value of Jungian psychology, and the questioning method."